Mind the Light, Katie

The History of Thirty-Three Female Lighthouse Keepers

Other lighthouse titles by the Cliffords

Women Who Kept the Lights: An Illustrated History of Female Lighthouse Keepers

Nineteenth-Century Lights: Historic Images of American Lighthouses

Maine Lighthouses: Documentation of Their Past

Mind the Light, Katie

The History of Thirty-Three Female Lighthouse Keepers

Mary Louise Clifford

J. Candace Clifford

Cypress Communications

Alexandria, Virginia

2006

Printed in the United States of America by Kirby Lithographic Company, Inc., Arlington, Virginia

10   9   8   7   6   5   4   3   2   1

ISBN 0-9636412-7-1

Front cover: *Oil painting created expressly for this book by artist Susie Gach Peelle of Locust Valley, New York, who retains the copyright.*

Published by Cypress Communications, 35 E. Rosemont Avenue, Alexandria, VA 22301; web site: <www.lighthousehistory.info>; email: <jcclifford@earthlink.net>

Table of Contents ↝

Author's Note ᣔ

Our book *Women Who Kept the Lights: An Illustrated History of Female Lighthouse Keepers* has been so popular that we offer here a condensed version for younger readers. The 140 women who served as principal keeper for more than a year are listed in the longer book. The 33 women presented here are those whose lives were recorded in logs, journals, official correspondence, newspaper articles and obituaries, and recollections by their children and grandchildren.

This is not a history of lighthouses. You can find history in our book *Nineteenth Century Lights: Historic Images of American Lighthouses,* particularly in the introductory sections to each of the four parts of that book.

Rather than explaining terms and titles as we go along, we include an extensive glossary at the end of this volume. Consult it when you find an unfamiliar term.

The United States has 40,580 miles of coastline and river channels and some 600 historic light stations, each of which once had a resident keeper. All of them are inventoried on the National Park Service's web site at <www.cr.nps.gov/maritime/ltsum.htm>.

Enjoy.

Mary Louise Clifford

J. Candace Clifford

I. Hannah Thomas at Gurnet Point Light Station, Massachusetts, 1775-1790 ॐ

When John Thomas told his wife in 1775 that he was raising a regiment to go and fight the British, she must have said, "But what about the lighthouse?"

Perhaps he replied, "I know you can handle it, Hannah. And the fee for keeping the lights will be very useful to you while I am gone."

Several years earlier John Thomas had been asked by a committee appointed by the General Court of Massachusetts to build and support a lighthouse on land he owned on Gurnet Point. That long narrow spit of land formed the protective northern arm around Plymouth Harbor. The agreement was recorded in Plymouth County courthouse on February 23, 1769.

Massachusetts Bay Colony paid Thomas rent of five shillings for his land and £200 a year to act as keeper of the lighthouse. In 1771 John Thomas's account of the expenses for Gurnet Point Light for the period of November 14, 1770, to November 14, 1771, included "40 measures of cotton weak [wick] yarn, £6.13.4; 50 measures of Candles, £1.133.4; one Lanthorn, 6 shillings; Carting of sundry items, £1.3; and a tin pail for carrying oil, 8 shillings."

Later correspondence gave the dimensions of the light: "The old Light House was of Wood 30 by 18 feet and 22 feet high, there were two lights raised 18 feet on Octagons at the ends of the Building." Each small tower contained two lamps— America's first "twin lights." The lanterns were constructed of heavy wooden frames holding small, thick panes of glass. They protected the lamps against the weather. A mariner could see that these twin lights were different from the single Barnstable Light nearby. The two Gurnet Point lights could be lined up to give a mariner his ship's exact location at that one point.

A lighthouse keeper worked seven days a week. The lamps at Gurnet Point had to be lit and kept burning every night. By 1775 the tallow candles used in the earlier lanterns in the colonies had been abandoned. Their light was too feeble to be seen from any distance. At Gurnet Point four flat-wick lamps (also called bucket lamps) were used. Each had four large wicks that had to be trimmed every few hours to make them burn brightly.

The lamps burned whale oil, which gave off toxic smoke. The soot coated the lantern glass and dimmed the light. The oil in the lamps had to be replenished two or three times during the night and the glass wiped clean. At dawn, the lamps were put out and cleaned.

When John went off to war, Hannah saw to it that the lights were lit and kept burning every night during the first year of her husband's absence. The legislative records of the Massachusetts Bay Council contain her petition "praying for an allowance [for keeping] the Light House on the Gurnet at the entrance [of Plymouth Harbor] one year five months and Nine days [ending the] 23 Day of April 1775, at which time the Lights were Extinguished."

Nothing is known of Hannah Thomas's experiences through the long years of the War for Independence. After the first year, Hannah no longer lit the lamps because they might aid enemy ships.

The American colonists who declared independence in 1776 had no navy—a disadvantage throughout the Revolution. Hostile sailing ships of the British Navy, armed with cannon, prowled up and down the Atlantic coast. They attacked and captured unarmed commercial vessels. British naval commanders must have studied the dozen lonely lighthouses that marked the hazards and harbors. If those landmarks could be put out of commission, or better still, destroyed, then the colonists' commercial ships would be even easier to attack.

Replacement twin towers were built at Gurnet Point in Plymouth Harbor in 1842. Shown here in the 1850s. Courtesy of the National Archives, #26-LG-7-11.

A garrison was stationed on Gurnet Point to protect the lighthouse. People living nearby built a crude fort around the twin towers to protect them. Nevertheless, a gun battle with a stranded British frigate offshore damaged the walls of the lighthouse.

John Thomas never came home from the war. Appointed a brigadier-general and commander of the colonial army in Canada, he died there of smallpox.

Two years after the fighting ended, the Massachusetts legislature received a petition from Hannah Thomas. In the February Session in 1785 the legislature granted a second petition, stating that the "benefit and privileges of keeping and tending the light house on an island called the Gurnet, at the entrance of Plymouth harbor, is reserved to the said John, Hannah, and John [their son], owners of the said island . . . ." Hannah asked that she be given "the barrack [erected] on her land at the Gurnet . . . for the damages done to her house, fences, etc., while a garrison was kept at that place."

Widowed and needing money to raise her children, Hannah continued in the role of lighthouse keeper. Although many lighthouses after the war were put in the hands of veterans, records for the years 1786 through 1789 show that Hannah was still in charge, paid £80 a year by the Massachusetts government. She also hired male helpers. In 1786 Nathaniel Burges signed a document, witnessed by her two sons, agreeing to "tend and keep the lighthouse situated on the Gurnet socalled, and at all proper times to light the lamps and keep the same lighted, in all respects faithfully to discharge the duty of a lighthouse keeper."

The ninth law passed by the new Congress in 1789 created the lighthouse establishment—one of the earliest public works in our country. In 1790 the new federal government took over all the lighthouses on the Atlantic coast, including Gurnet Point. The U.S. Lighthouse Establishment was assigned to the Treasury Department. Every contract, large or small, as well as the appointment and salary of every keeper, was personally approved by President Washington.

A single tower stood at Gurnet Point in 1958, surrounded by traces of Revolutionary War earthworks. Courtesy of the U.S. Coast Guard.

On March 19, 1790, Superintendent of Lighthouses Benjamin Lincoln wrote Alexander Hamilton, Secretary of the Treasury, as follows:

> Mrs. Thomas, the widow of the late General Thomas, . . . has been considered the keeper of the lighthouse at Plymouth. The house stands on her land . . .. The man who keeps the lighthouse for her has trouble with the improvement of the island. This however, is a private bargain between Mrs. Thomas and the keeper.

John Thomas [Hannah's son] went to Lighthouse Superintendent Lincoln in 1790 asking to be appointed keeper at Gurnet. Mr. Lincoln wrote the Secretary of the Treasury as follows:

> I have now with me Mr. Thomas, son of the late General Thomas, whose mother has the care of the lighthouse at Plymouth. When she was first appointed to that trust, he was a minor; otherwise he probably would have had the appointment himself. He is a young gentleman of good character and I think is a fair candidate for the appointment under the United states.

In 1801 the lighthouse at Gurnet Point burned. The land on which it was built still belonged to the Thomas family. Congress appropriated $2,500 in 1802 to buy the land and erect new towers. The Thomas family received $120 for the land on which the lighthouse stood. The towers were rebuilt again in 1842.

Although the need for twin towers was eventually eliminated by better optics, two lights were maintained at Gurnet Point long after most others were abandoned. Not until 1924 was one of them discontinued and the tower removed. The second tower survives and continues as an active aid to navigation.

Much of the information in this chapter comes from copies of documents in the private collection of Richard M. Boonisar. Also from National Archives Record Group 26, "Letters Received by the Treasury Department, 1785-1812" and "Lighthouse Letters, 1792-1809."

Black Rock Light Station off Bridgeport, Connecticut, around 1880. Kate Moore assisted her father there from 1817 until 1871, then served as official keeper from 1871 until 1879. The 1823 tower still stands. Courtesy of the National Archives, #26-LG-11-3.

II. Catherine Moore at Black Rock Light Station, Connecticut, 1817-1879 ✎

Catherine (Kate) Moore did not become official keeper of the Black Rock Light on the north shore of Long Island Sound until 1871, when she was 76 years old. She went to live there, however, in 1817, when her father, Stephen Tomlinson Moore, won the keeper's post after injuries from a fall aboard ship kept him from going back to sea.

In 1889 Kate told a reporter from the *New York Sunday World*, "I was just 12 years old when I first began to assist my father in trimming the wicks. A few years after that his health began to fail and from then on I was practically the keeper." She did her invalid father's work and cared for him for 54 years.

Kate's is the first voice to come directly to us from the ranks of women who kept the lights. "It was a miserable [light] to keep going, nothing like those in use nowadays," she said of the fixed white light. "It consisted of eight oil lamps which took four gallons of oil each night, and if they were not replenished at stated intervals all through the night, they went out. During very windy nights it was almost impossible to keep them burning at all, and I had to stay there all night."

During the early 1800s, lighthouse lamps burned whale oil—a thick strain in the summer, a thinner strain in the winter. In cold weather, even the thinner oil tended to congeal. The keeper either carried heated oil to the lantern or kept a fire burning in a warming stove in the lantern of the lighthouse.

The brightness of the light depended on how well the wicks were trimmed. All the accumulated soot had to be polished off the reflectors every day so that they would intensify the light. Mariners depended on the lights to warn them away from shoals and ledges. Sailors in those days navigated by watching the sun and the stars and by using simple compasses. They watched the tides, wind direction, water surfaces, cloud formations, and bird behavior to predict weather.

Kate's light was located on Fayerweather Island, three scraggly acres of tall grasses and ailanthus trees (planted by Kate). "On [calm] nights I slept at home, dressed in a suit of boy's clothes, my lighted lantern hanging at my headboard and my face turned so that I could see shining on the wall the light from the tower and know if anything had happened."

If the light went out, Kate got up to tend to it. "Our house was forty rods (a little over 213 yards) from the lighthouse, and to reach it I had to walk across two planks under which on stormy nights were four feet of water. And it was not too easy to stay on those slippery, wet boards with the wind whirling and the spray blinding me."

Storms and gales were part of her life. "The island has been ruined by gales a number of times. Every fifty years these great gales come, the waves dashing clear over the island, and on Jan. 19, 1820, the last of the old trees [on the island] was swept away. The lighthouse itself blew over once when I was there."

On September 4, 1821, her father wrote a barely legible letter to the superintendent of lights announcing that disaster:

> This is to inform you that the light hous on fayweather Island blew down last Night and Brok most of it to pieces. The Corper & lamps are all Spilt. One But of Oil part full went [page damaged]. The rest it has Broke and mash the top so Bad that it apears to be split. I am Employed in Giten the Corper and Iron in to the Volt [vault].

Kate echoed his words. "It was a dreadful thing to have happen, for this was then the only light on the Connecticut side of Long Island Sound—the only light between New Haven and Eaton Neck—and was of course of inestimable value to mariners. Sometimes there were more than 200 sailing vessels in here at night, and some nights there were as many as three or four wrecks . . .."

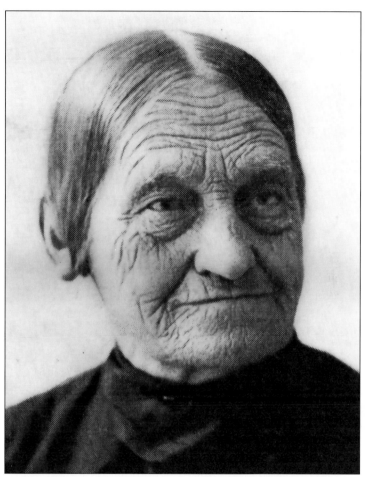

Kate Moore at age 94, after her retirement as keeper of the Black Rock Light off Bridgeport, Connecticut. Courtesy of Historical Collections, Bridgeport Public Library.

In the 72 years she was at Black Rock Light, Kate Moore saved at least 21 lives. "I wish it had been double that number. Of course there were a great many others, washed up on the shore, half-dead, whom we revived, and they all stayed with us until they received means to leave. They used to eat our provisions and the Government never paid us a cent for boarding them."

Dead sailors washed up on the shore as well. "Hundreds!" Kate said. "We had to keep them, too, until the Government chose to dispose of them."

When asked whether she was lonely, Kate said that she had never known any other life. "I never had much time to get lonely. I had a lot of poultry and two cows to care for, and each year raised twenty sheep, doing the shearing myself—and the killing when necessary. You see, in the winter you couldn't get to land on account of the ice being too thin, or the water too rough. Then in the summer I had my garden to make and keep. I raised all my own stuff, and as we had to depend on rain for our water, quite a bit of the time was consumed looking after that. We tried a number of times to dig for water, but always struck salt."

Kate did not consider her life unusually hard. "You see, I had done all this for so many years, and I knew no other life, so I was sort of fitted for it. I never had much of a childhood, as other children have it. That is, I never knew playmates. Mine were the chickens, ducks and lambs and my two Newfoundland dogs."

Kate never went to school, but she learned to read and collected a library of a hundred books—some given to her by visitors to the island. She also carried on a thriving business planting, seeding, and gathering oysters in Long Island Sound.

Kate also carved duck decoys, selling them to visitors as souvenirs or to hunters. "I just took two blocks of wood and carved them out with a knife. It didn't take long to make one, and I liked to do it. I often worked at them in the nights when I had to stay up."

Kate Moore tended the Black Rock Light until she was 83 years old. When she retired in 1878, she owned a house and had $75,000 in a bank account. She lived to age 105.

This chapter is based on an 1889 article in the New York Sunday World; *Ivan Justinius,* History of Black Rock *(Bridgeport: Anoniak Printing Service, Inc., 1955); Pat Jordan, "The Keeper of Black Rock Light" in* The New England Sampler II *(Concord, New Hampshire: 1971); and an article in the* Bridgeport Standard, *March 25, 1878.*

III. Rebecca Flaherty at Sand Key Light Station, Florida, 1830-1837 ॐ

Rebecca Flaherty wrote many letters. In 1824 she wrote a long letter to Stephen Pleasonton, the Treasury Department official in charge of lighthouses, seeking a keeper's appointment for her husband John. She explained that he had "served his Country in the hour of danger and more particularly in the glorious defense of Baltimore" during the War of 1812. She believed that the Southern climate would help his rheumatism, and she hoped that the lighthouse at Pensacola, Florida, might be available for him.

Appointments of lighthouse keepers were still submitted to the President of the United States for approval. In 1825 Rebecca wrote a long letter (apparently not her first) to Mrs. Adams, the wife of President John Quincy Adams:

> Sensible of your philanthropy, I presume once more to trouble you respecting a situation for my husband. There is a light house at Thomsons [Thomas] Point near Annapolis that is nearly ready for the keeper to go into, and if you would please to grant us your interest with Mr. Stephen Pleasonton, the 5th auditor, I feel confident we could obtain the situation. My husband can get letters here from gentlemen of the first standing, and if you will kindly condescend to give him a letter, that alone would have much more weight than all the rest.

What action Mrs. Adams took is unknown, but Rebecca's lengthy correspondence in our National Archives indicates that Major John Flaherty of Baltimore received the keeper's appointment at Dry Tortugas Light Station off the coast of

Rebecca Flaherty went with her husband to the Florida Keys when he was assigned to keep the first tower on Dry Tortugas on Garden Key in 1826. Courtesy of the U.S. Coast Guard.

Florida in the spring of 1826. A revenue cutter transported his family and household effects to the island.

By November of that year, Pleasonton reported to the Secretary of the Treasury that the Flahertys had problems:

> . . . they are nearly destitute of all the necessities of life, and . . . they have not the means, of themselves, to obtain a supply to relieve them from a situation so disturbing and appalling. I have respectfully to request that you will give orders to the Revenue Boat on the Charleston station to proceed forthwith to the Dry Tortugas, with such articles of provisions & stores, for their immediate use and preservation . . ..

In 1827 Major Flaherty was transferred to Sand Key Light nine miles from Key West. He took his wife and five children to live in the small house next to the tower. The nearby Key West Light was a fixed light. To distinguish Sand Key from that light, a revolving light was placed in the lantern at Sand Key atop a 70-foot conical brick tower. Fourteen lamps with 21-inch reflectors behind them were hung on a chandelier, and on a clear night could be seen far out to sea.

In 1828 Rebecca wrote a letter to Stephen Pleasonton informing him that her husband was ill and should see a doctor. She asked for a six-month leave of absence. She herself was not well. "The climate does not agree with either of us. I hope Sir, you will not think us whimsical, you were so kind as to have us moved to Sand Key to better our situation which it did, and nothing but the loss of our health could induce me to wish [John] to resign."

Major Flaherty died in 1830. Rebecca, already experienced in tending the light at Sand Key, was appointed keeper.

In 1833, Rebecca wrote again to the Secretary of the Treasury:

> I solicit your aid in correcting many of the grievances to which I am exposed in discharging [my] duties . . . Sand Key is nine miles from Key West, and such is the violence of the seas for days and weeks together, as to render any intercourse with that place extremely precarious. A boat has generally been furnished by the Government for my use, but it has been constructed to draw too much water, . . . mak[ing] it impossible to shelter it from the injury and damage which is effected by the commotion of the sea. On the East side of Sand Key there is a good harbour; which—if the Government would build a center board boat, drawing from six to nine inches water—would at all times, and during the greatest gale, protect it from all damage.

She added that the station boat was too damaged to be used, "exposing her to starvation." In addition to needing a new boat, she wanted a man hired to operate the boat and bring needed provisions from Key West. In the same letter she complained that the government had paid for her firewood since 1827, but that a new regulation had stopped the payments.

In 1831 an attorney in Key West, William Randolph Hackley, included in his diary a description of Sand Key. He said that Rebecca Flaherty, her sister, and a hired man were the only inhabitants of the key, which he described as 150 to 200 yards long and 50 yards wide—the size of two football fields.

On November 22, 1834, *The Florida Herald*, a St. Augustine newspaper, reported a special celebration on Sand Key: "Mrs. R. F. Flaherty, formerly of Fredrick City, Maryland . . . was married to Captain Fredrick Neill . . . at the Sand Key Lighthouse." Rebecca Flaherty Neill remained keeper of the Sand Key light until 1837, when Captain Joshua Appleby took her place.

Sources for this chapter include National Archives Record Group 26, Entries 17F, 17G, 17H, 82; Love Dean, Lighthouses of the Florida Keys *(Sarasota, Florida: Pineapple Press, 1998).*

IV. Barbara Mabrity, 1832-1864, and Mary Elizabeth Bethel, 1908-1913, at Key West Light Station, Florida ɜʋ

Florida was added to the United States in 1820. A naval base was established on Key West in 1823, and construction began on a lighthouse in 1825. Michael Mabrity, formerly a coast pilot, became its first keeper. His wife Barbara was appointed his assistant. He continued to serve as a part-time harbor pilot and was a member of the town council in 1828. He died of yellow fever in 1832, leaving Barbara and six children. Barbara took over his duties and tended the 15 whale-oil lamps until 1858, when a Fresnel lens was installed.

Indian wars in Florida between 1835 and 1842 caused the Navy to strengthen its base on Key West. A road was built close to the lighthouse "to make it easier to spot possible Indians in the woods." The road gave Barbara Mabrity easier access to the town. In 1845 a fort was begun close to the lighthouse, one of a string designed to protect the nation's major ports. It gave Barbara some sense of security.

Nature, however, was the greater threat. Barbara Mabrity survived four hurricanes—in 1835, 1841, 1842, and 1846. U.S. Navy Lieutenant William C. Pease, aboard a small vessel in the harbor, described the storm:

> The air was full of water, and no man could look windward for a second. . . . wrecks of all descriptions: one ship on her beam, three brigs dismasted, also three schooners; three vessels sunk, . . . four vessels bottom up. How many persons attached to these vessels I am unable to say. We picked up only two. The lighthouse at Key West and Sand Key washed away, and Key West is in

ruins. A white sand beach covers the spot where Key West lighthouse stood, and waves roll over the spot where Sand Key was.

Barbara Mabrity was 64 years old at the time. The destroyed lighthouse was replaced on a hill further inland and on higher ground. There she lived and worked in the small, prefabricated, one-and-a-half-story, wooden keeper's dwelling for another 16 years. In 1850 an assistant was appointed to help her with the buoys that had been placed on the treacherous reefs surrounding the island. In 1858 a third-order Fresnel lens was installed, using a single lard-oil hydraulic lamp with three circular wicks. Keeping this new lamp clean was much less work.

Key West was the only lighthouse in Florida that remained under Union control and was kept lit throughout the Civil War. In 1864, Barbara Mabrity was accused of favoring the South and was encouraged to retire. She refused, and was then removed from her position. She died three years later at age 85.

Barbara Mabrity was honored in 1999 when the Coast Guard named the second of a new series of keeper-class buoy tenders after her.

The second tower for Key West Light Station was built in 1847. Shown here before it was raised 20 feet in 1894, the station was deactivated in 1969 and is now a museum. Photo courtesy of the U.S. Coast Guard.

Mary Elizabeth Bethel served both as assistant and head keeper at Key West. Photo courtesy of Monroe County Library.

William Bethel became keeper at Key West Light Station in 1889. In 1891 his wife Mary Elizabeth was appointed acting assistant keeper. In 1908, after her husband fell ill, Mary Elizabeth received the keeper's appointment, with her son Merrill as assistant keeper.

In the hurricane of 1909 the glass in the lantern came crashing down just as Mary Elizabeth was about to climb the stairs in the tower. She remained at her post until 1913, when the light was automated.

This chapter uses Thomas Taylor, "The First Key West Lighthouse" in The Keeper's Log, *spring 1995, and "The Second Key West Lighthouse," summer 1995; National Archives Record Group 26, Entry 17H; Love Dean,* Lighthouses of the Florida Keys *(Sarasota, Florida: Pineapple Press, 1998); and Walter C. Maloney,* A Sketch of the History of Key West, Florida *(Gainesville: University of Florida Press, 1968).*

Bombay Hook Light Station in 1897. Courtesy of the National Archives, #26-LG-10-13B.

V. Margaret Stuart at Bombay Hook Light Station, Delaware, 1850-1862 ⌀

No words come directly from Margaret Stuart. She kept the Bombay Hook Light Station on the south side of the Smyrna River near the shore of the Delaware River from 1850 to 1862. The white brick, two-story dwelling was surmounted by a short tower and lantern room in the center of the roof.

Margaret's father, Duncan Stuart, was its first keeper. The appointment passed to Margaret in 1850. The lighthouse inspector reported in 1851 that Mr. Stuart was 89 years old, and that his daughters did the actual work of keeping the station "neat and clean."

The inspector's report indicated that the Stuarts were tending Argand lamps under rather difficult conditions:

> Reflectors of thin copper and a very thin film of silver-plating, much worn off in spots; not firmly placed on the frame, and easily put out of adjustment. Lantern small, glass 8 x 12 inches; sashes thick and black—want painting very much; the frame of the dome and the lantern very dirty for want of paint, lantern leaks very much; until rebuilt, leaked in every part of building; tower so open it is difficult to carry a light into the lantern; wood-work rough and not planed; floor of lantern coppered . . ..

The inspector reported that Mr. Stuart had the lighthouse whitewashed at his own expense because there was no allowance for lime for whitewashing. The report made the dwelling sound rather primitive:

> House wants painting; spouts, etc., rusty for want of paint. Roof of the house very open—places a quarter of an inch between the shingles, brick-work rough; floors not tongued and grooved; rough and open in the attics; garret

rooms not plastered; wooden pillar, supporting steps, much worm-eaten; cellar in bad order—wants cementing and repairs; kitchen in cellar; oil smells baldly [badly].

In 1855 the *Annual Report of the Light-House Board* indicated that "new iron lanterns for fourth-order apparatus have been substituted for the old and defective style hitherto in use," and "superior French plate glass of very large dimensions" installed in the lantern. These should have made Margaret's duties much easier.

Margaret Stuart's appointment ended, as did that of many other lighthouse keepers, during the Civil War. Many lights were extinguished then to prevent their aiding the enemy. The confusion of the period affected the careers of many keepers.

The site where the lighthouse stood is now part of the Bombay Hook Wildlife Refuge.

Sources for this chapter include Robert deGast, The Lighthouses of the Chesapeake *(Baltimore: Johns Hopkins University Press, 1973); and U.S. Fish and Wildlife Service,* A Brief History of Bombay Hook National Wildlife Refuge *(Smyrna, Delaware: no date).*

VI. Abbie Burgess Grant at Matinicus Rock Light Station, 1853-1872, and at Whitehead Light Station, Maine, 1875-1890 ᧏

Abbie Burgess was never a head keeper, but she is famous in New England lighthouse lore. In 1853 she was 14 years old when her family moved to the light station on Matinicus Rock off the coast of Maine. She helped her father tend 28 Argand lamps, which hung from a circular chandelier. Her mother was an invalid. Abbie had an older brother, Benji, who was generally away on fishing boats. Abbie was the eldest of three sisters. She took her turn tending the lights and the stove during the night, so that her father could spend part of his time fishing for lobsters and sailing to Rockland to sell them.

Matinicus Rock is a lonely, barren outcropping five miles off the south end of Matinicus Island. The mainland is 20 miles away. Two stone towers were built in 1848 to hold the lamps. They were attached to both ends of the rectangular rubblestone keeper's dwelling. Matinicus Rock had small structures for a fogbell and other equipment. Sheds housed coal to provide heat, the oil used to fuel the lamps, and lifeboats. A cistern or rain shed collected fresh water.

The island's surface was a confused plain of loose stones and boulders, over which waves swept at high tide. In heavy weather the rocks and shoals around Matinicus Rock were extreme hazards to sailing ships. Any failure of the light for even a short time could lead to disaster.

In 1855 the lighthouse tender, which brought supplies twice a year, failed to make its regular September call. By

Matinicus Rock Light Station off the coast of Maine. Courtesy of the U.S. Coast Guard.

January supplies were running desperately low. Keeper Burgess decided to sail to Matinicus Island to fetch food for his family and medicine for his sick wife. His son was away fishing, so Abbie was left in charge of the light. Soon after Burgess left, a storm blew in out of the northeast. He was unable to return for four weeks.

Sheets of spray crashed over the island, driven by sleet and snow. As the violence of the gale increased, Abbie moved her mother and younger sisters into one of the two light towers. Finally, at high tide, the waves washed completely over the island.

In a letter to a friend, Abbie gave a detailed description of that terrifying and exhausting month:

> You have often expressed a desire to view the sea out upon the ocean when it was angry. Had you been here on the 19 January, I surmise you would have been satisfied. Father was away. Early in the day, as the tide rose, the sea made a complete breach over the rock, washing every movable thing away, and of the old dwelling not one stone was left upon another of the foundation.
>
> The new dwelling was flooded and the windows [shutters] had to be secured to prevent the violence of the

Abbie Burgess may have been the inspiration for the artist's rendering on the cover of Harper's Young People: An Illustrated Weekly, *May 2, 1882. Courtesy of Virginia State Library and Archives.*

spray from breaking them in. As the tide came, the sea rose higher and higher, till the only endurable places were the light towers. If they stood we were saved, otherwise our fate was only too certain.

But for some reason, I know not why, I had no misgivings and went on with my work as usual. For four weeks, owing to rough weather, no landing could be effected on the Rock. During this time we were without assistance of any male member of our family. Though at times greatly exhausted by my labors, not once did the lights fail. Under God I was able to perform all my accustomed duties as well as my father's.

You know the hens were our only companions. Becoming convinced, as the gale increased, that unless they were brought into the house they would be lost, I said to mother: "I must try to save them." She advised me not to attempt it. The thought, however, of parting with them without an effort was not to be endured, so seizing a basket, I ran out a few yards after the rollers had passed and the sea fell off a little, with the water knee deep, to the coop, and rescued all but one. It was the work of a moment, and I was back in the house with the door fastened, but none too quick, for at that instant my little sister, standing at a window, exclaimed, "Oh, look! look there! the worst sea is coming!"

That wave destroyed the old dwelling and swept the Rock. I cannot think you would enjoy remaining here any great length of time for the sea is never still and when agitated, it roars, shuts out every other sound, even drowning our voices.

After the storm subsided, Abbie's father returned to find his family and the lights safe. A year later, under similar conditions, he was away from the rock for three weeks, but Abbie kept the lights burning. This time the family ran out of food. They were down to a daily ration of one egg and one cup of corn meal when Burgess returned.

In 1860 Abbie's father lost his position to a Republican appointee. Abbie stayed on to assist the new keeper. She fell in love with his son Isaac Grant. After they married, Abbie acted as Isaac's assistant when he became keeper of Matinicus, receiving a $440 annual salary.

Whitehead Light Station on Penobscot Bay in Maine. Courtesy of the National Archives, # 26-LG-4-37.

Raising four children, Abbie and her husband remained on Matinicus until 1875, when they were transferred to Whitehead Light, near Spruce Head, Maine. There Abbie's salary as assistant keeper was increased to $480 annually. She and her husband kept the lights at Whitehead until 1890. Abbie's poor health led both of them to resign. She died two years later, having spent 37 of her 53 years in lighthouses.

In 1998 the Coast Guard commissioned the 175-foot buoy tender *Abbie Burgess* with an 18-man crew, which services nearly 400 aids to navigation between Pemaquid Point, Maine, and the Canadian border.

Sources for this chapter include personal correspondence with Patricia Grant of Augusta, Maine, Abbie's great-granddaughter, and with David Gamage of Wilton, Maine, grandson of a keeper at Whitehead Light Station; Robert Carse, Keepers of the Lights: A History of American Lighthouses *(New York: Charles Scribner's Sons, 1969); and U.S. Coast Guard press release No. 083-98.*

Biloxi Light Station on the Gulf of Mexico, kept by Mary Reynolds from 1854 to 1866, by Maria Younghans from 1867 to 1918, and by Miranda Younghans from 1919 to 1929. Courtesy of the National Archives, #26-LG-34-22A.

Biloxi Lighthouse currently sits on the median strip of U.S. Highway 90. Courtesy of the U.S. Coast Guard.

VII. Mary Reynolds, 1854-1866, Maria Younghans, 1867-1918, and Miranda Younghans, 1919-1929, at Biloxi Light Station, Mississippi ᠌

Women tended the light at Biloxi, Mississippi, longer than at any other light in the United States. Mary Reynolds was in charge from 1854 to 1866. She was followed by Maria Younghans, keeper from 1867 to 1918. Maria's daughter Miranda followed her and held her post until 1929. Together these three women racked up three-quarters of a century of continuous and dedicated service. Yet almost no personal information about them has been uncovered.

Built in 1847, the Biloxi tower was prefabricated cast iron, with a balustrade encircling the watch room. The components were brought by ship to the permanent location. If necessary, cast-iron towers can be disassembled and moved.

Biloxi's three-second flashing light marked the entrance to the city's harbor for the many schooners that plied the Mississippi Sound and Gulf waters in search of shrimp and oysters. Other schooners carried lumber on the Tchouticabouffa River and other inland waterways.

To obtain her appointment in 1854, Mary Reynolds sought the aid of Mississippi's newly elected senator, Albert Gallatin Brown. She was the second keeper of the Biloxi Light. Her annual salary was $400.

When the Civil War broke out, the patriots of Biloxi extinguished the light so that it could not aid Yankee ships. Mary Reynolds worried about her responsibility for the federal stores in her possession. In 1861 she wrote to the governor for assistance in influencing the local men:

. . . I have for several years past been the Keeper of the Light House at Biloxi, the small salary accruing from which has helped me to support a large family of orphaned children.

. . . I do not know if my [federal] salary as the Keeper of the Light House will be continued.

On the 18th of June last, the citizens of Biloxi ordered the light to be extinguished which was immediately done and shortly after others came and demanded the key of the Light Tower which has ever since remained in the hands of a Company calling themselves "Home Guards."

At the time they took possession of the Tower it contained valuable Oil, the quantity being marked on my books. I have on several occasions seen disreputable characters taking out the oil in bottles. Today they carried away a large stone jug capable of containing several gallons. They may take also in the night as no one here appeared to have any authority over them.

Their Captain, J. Fewell, is also Mayor of the City of Biloxi, and if you would have the kindness to write him orders to have the oil measured and placed under my charge at the dwelling of the Light House I would be very grateful to you for so doing.

. . . I have ever faithfully performed the duties of Light Keeper in storm and sunshine attending it. I ascended the Tower at and after the last destructive storm (1860) when men stood appalled at the danger I encountered. . . .

The governor's reply is not available, but the mayor replied to the collector of customs as follows:

At your request I have the honor to inform you that the Citizens of Biloxi in a public meeting resolved to remove the Reflector from the Light House at this place, and to take possession of the Oil in possession of the late Keeper, which was sold for the amount of Thirty Dollars which fund was distributed by me to the poor destitute families. The property which the Citizens have taken from the premises of the Light House is safely secured and is subject to the order of the authorities of the Confederate States Government.

Mary Reynolds was listed as official keeper until 1866—although the light may have remained dark until that year. Like many Southern keepers, she was paid by the Confederate

Light-House Establishment during the war. Her name reappears in the records of the U.S. Light-House Board as keeper of the Pass Christian Light on the Mississippi Sound from 1873 to 1874.

Perry Younghans succeeded Mary Reynolds as keeper of the Biloxi Light. Owner of a nearby brick yard that had been destroyed by northern forces, he used political influence to obtain his appointment after the war. He died within the year. His wife Maria assumed her husband's duties and continued at her post until 1918, winning the highest approval from the inspectors for her work. Little remains to illuminate Maria's half-century-long career. Annual reports of the Light-House Board mention only changes and repairs made to the property

A few newspaper clippings give tiny glimpses of her life. An 1893 edition of the New Orleans *Daily Picayune*, reporting on a hurricane, stated that "Mrs. (Maria) Younghans, the plucky woman who was in charge of the Biloxi light, kept a light going all through the storm, notwithstanding that there were several feet of water in the room where she lived."

In the Biloxi and Gulfport *Daily Herald* of August 22, 1925, an obituary states that Maria Younghans "in the winter of 1870 called her brother-in-law, and effected through him the rescue of a man being swept out to sea about daylight, clinging to an upturned boat; and during the 1916 storm, when the heavy glass in the lighthouse tower was broken by a large pelican being blown against it, she and her daughter, mindful of the especial need of the light on such a night, replaced the glass temporarily and made the 'light to shine' as before, unimpaired."

As Maria aged, her daughter Miranda acted as her assistant, taking over many of her duties, and assuming all of them when Maria retired. A female assistant keeper, Edna Holley, was appointed to help Maria. The light was electrified in 1926, during Miranda's tenure. She retired in 1929.

The Biloxi and Gulfport *Daily Herald* carried Miranda's obituary on February 6, 1933, noting that "her unfailing courtesy and dignity gave hundreds of casual visitors to the light house a beautiful memory of her, and a visit to the light

*Miranda Younghans, who
kept the Biloxi Light Station
from 1919 until 1929.
Courtesy of Murella H.
Powell Local History &
Genealogy Collection, Biloxi
Public Library.*

house was always described with many references to Miss
Younghans."

In the mid-20th century the Biloxi Light was automated
and the tower deeded to the city. It is now a private aid to
navigation. The keeper's quarters were destroyed by hurricane
Camille in 1969. The tower survived hurricane Katrina in 2005
although surrounding buildings were leveled.

*Sources for this chapter include Mississippi Department of Archives and
History, Series E, Volume 54, Pettus; M. James Stevens, "Biloxi's Lady
Lighthouse Keeper" in* The Journal of Mississippi History, *date unknown;
National Archives Record Group 365, Treasury Department Collection of
Confederate Records, E 78 (provided by Sandra Clunies); Murella Powell
of the Harrison County Library System; Curator of Historic Facilities, Tullis-
Toledano Manor, Biloxi; and articles by Kat Bergeron in the* Sun/Herald,
April 1, 1984.

VIII. Charlotte Layton, 1856-1860, and Emily Fish, 1893-1914, at Point Pinos Light Station, California; Juliet Nichols at Angel Island Light Station, California, 1902-1914 ॐ

In 1855 Charles Layton, an army veteran, became first keeper of Point Pinos Light Station at the entrance to Monterey Bay—the oldest continuously operating lighthouse on the West Coast. He brought his wife Charlotte, three sons, and one daughter to the drab Cape Cod bungalow with the light tower in the center of its roof. That same year Layton was killed while serving as a member of a sheriff's posse chasing a notorious outlaw.

The local collector of customs, who was also superintendent of lighthouses, wrote the Light-House Board in Washington, D.C., as follows:

> Charlotte A. Layton and four children have been left entirely destitute. I authorized her to continue at the post occupied by her late husband, and she is now discharging all the duties of principal keeper of the Lights at Point Pinos. I take much pleasure in recommending her for the place of principal keeper: she is a person eminently qualified for the position: she is industrious and bears an unblemished reputation.

Enclosed was a petition signed by a group of citizens in Monterey. "You will have the goodness," the collector of customs wrote, "to present the memorial to the Hon. Secretary of the Treasury and urge the confirmation of the appointment." The appointment followed promptly in 1856.

The lamp Charlotte tended burned whale oil, forced up from a tank by a gravity-operated piston. Its beam was concentrated by a third-order Fresnel lens manufactured in France. A falling-weight mechanism rotated a metal shutter around the light, causing the beam to be cut off to seaward 10 out of every 30 seconds. The weights were wound by hand like a clock.

Charlotte Layton was paid $1,000 a year, a salary much higher than that of keepers on the East Coast. The supply of available labor in California lagged behind demand. Men outnumbered women twelve to one, but the men were prospecting for gold, giving women a wider range of employment opportunities. Charlotte had a male assistant keeper who earned $800. In 1860 Charlotte married her assistant, George Harris. Although the Lighthouse Service permitted a man to be supervised by a woman, Charlotte stepped down to again become assistant keeper. By 1870 they had retired. Charlotte died in 1896.

1859 drawing of the Point Pinos Light Station in Pacific Grove, California, after an 1855 sketch by Major Hartman Bach. Courtesy of the National Archives, #26-LG-66-64.

Three decades later, Point Pinos Light Station had another female keeper, this one not of the working class. In 1893 widowed Emily Fish introduced to the modest Cape Cod bungalow a Chinese servant and furnishings seldom seen in a lighthouse—antique furniture, good paintings, fine china and old silver, leather-bound books. The servant had come with Emily from China when her husband gave up his consular post there. The furnishings came from the elegant house in Oakland where she and her husband had lived after he established a private medical practice and began teaching at the University of California.

Emily was 50 when her husband died. Her naval officer son-in-law was Inspector of the 12th District of the Lighthouse Service. He mentioned casually one day that the keeper of the Point Pinos Light Station was about to retire. Emily decided she would like the post. Her son-in-law arranged her appointment.

Point Pinos Light Station included 92 acres of sand and scrub. After transforming the keeper's house, Emily had topsoil brought in and spread so she could plant trees, grass, and a cypress hedge around the yard. Then she added Thoroughbred horses to pull her carriage. Holstein cows grazed around the station, white leghorn chickens provided eggs, French poodles greeted visitors. After her mourning period ended, Emily began giving small dinner parties for artists and writers and naval officers from ships calling in Monterey Bay.

Authorized to employ laborers to help with the heavy work around the station, Emily listed in her log more than 30 male workers during her years as keeper. She noted that most of them were discharged for incompetence. Inspectors invariably reported that the Point Pinos Light Station was in excellent condition.

The inspector who had arranged Emily Fish's appointment was married to her niece. Emily had raised Juliet as her own child and seen her married to Lt. Commander Henry E. Nichols. After his service as Lighthouse Inspector, Commander Nichols was sent to the Philippines and died in 1898 during the Spanish-American War. As the wife of a former Lighthouse Service officer, Juliet was offered the

Emily A. Fish, who kept the Point Pinos Light in Pacific Grove, California, from 1893 to 1914. Courtesy of Monterey Public Library, California History Room.

keeper's post at the Angel Island Light in San Francisco Bay in 1902. She tended a fogbell and an uncovered fifth-order lens with a fixed red light, which was moved by pulley out of the bell house each evening.

Emily Fish and Juliet Nichols were both on duty at their respective lighthouses early on the morning of April 18, 1906. They experienced firsthand one of the world's most severe earthquakes. Emily was making her final rounds around 5 a.m. when she heard the horses in the barn pounding the floor and the cows lowing uneasily. She went to the watch room to scan the landscape, hoping to find whatever was disturbing the animals.

Emily wrote in her log that the first tremor of the "violent and continued earthquake" jarred the lighthouse at 5:13 a.m.

The building shook and swayed, while cracking noises and tinkling sounds of breaking glass came from the tower. Outside the window, trees whipped and swayed.

The noises, the shaking of the earth, and the trembling of the building lasted for about two minutes. Emily noted that a crack in the brickwork and coping of the tower was much enlarged. In the lantern the shock had bent a connecting tube and jarred the damper so that the lamp flame had run up much higher than it should. The violent tremors continued as she fought to control the flame.

When the shaking finally ended, she surveyed the whole station to assess the damage. In the lantern, the prisms in the Fresnel lens had been jarred and had struck against each other, making the tinkling sound she had heard. The granite walls of the lighthouse withstood the shocks, but the water in the woodhouse tank was splashed out on the floor. When Emily tried to report the damage to the district office in San Francisco, she found all telegraphic and telephone communication cut off. The train track was also obstructed so no trains were running.

The 1906 Annual Report of the Light-House Board reported that "the damage was so great that it became necessary to tear down and rebuild the tower with reinforced concrete." In 1907 the repairs were completed.

Juliet Nichols was at her post on Angel Island in San Francisco Bay on that fateful day in 1906. She was making a final check of her equipment when she heard a rumbling sound. She looked across the water to the city silhouetted against the hills and was astonished to see buildings on the waterfront collapsing. Snatching her field glasses, she watched, horrified, as familiar landmarks crumbled into piles of rubble. As the tremors continued, fires broke out. They raged through factories, homes, and office buildings, until the skyline was blackened with smoke and ash.

Isolated on her island, Juliet watched helplessly as the tragedy unfolded before her eyes. Later she would learn that the earthquake had damaged every community within 100 miles of San Francisco.

Fogbell ringing mechanism in Hooper Strait Lighthouse, Chesapeake Bay Maritime Museum, St. Michaels, Maryland. National Park Service photo by Candace Clifford.

Mechanical fog signals were notorious for breaking down. The mechanical pounding of the fogbell produced strong vibrations, which caused tension bars and hammer springs to break. Sometimes they snapped the rope attached to the clockwork weight.

Less than three months after the earthquake, Angel Island's new fog signal, less than a year old, broke down. Juliet was watching the fog roll in through the Golden Gate, as it so regularly does. She heard the foghorns start up in lighthouses on both sides of the channel. She rushed to start her own equipment, only to have the machinery cough into silence a few minutes later. She could see tips of the masts of a sailing vessel approaching through the fog. With no time for repairs, she grabbed a hammer and began pounding the bell, warning the ship away from her island. In her report on the malfunctioning of the equipment, she wrote that she pounded the bell at the prescribed intervals for 20 hours before the fog finally lifted.

Two days later the Angel Island machinery failed again, forcing Juliet to repeat her exhausting ordeal. When the weather cleared, she summoned the lighthouse engineer to make repairs. Juliet Nichols's whole career at Angel Island was a battle with fog. Her log recorded periods of fog as long as 80 hours at a time; during many of these incidents, she had to strike the bell by hand. Angel Island was one of the worst hazards in San Francisco Bay, and Juliet Nichols took her duties very seriously. She richly deserved the commendations she earned for her dedication.

In 1914 both women retired. Emily Fish bought a house in Pacific Grove, where she lived quietly until her death at age 88 in 1931. Juliet lived equally privately in the hills of Oakland until her death in 1947.

⋯⊷☰◑☰⊶⋯

Sources for this chapter include Annual Reports of the Light-House Board; Clifford Gallant, "Emily Fish, the Socialite Keeper" *in* The Keeper's Log, Spring 1985; *and files of the U. S. Lighthouse Society, San Francisco.*

Catherine Murdock, keeper of Rondout Creek Light Station on the Hudson River from 1857 to 1907. These woodcut illustrations appeared in the Kingston Daily Freeman *around 1888. Courtesy of the Rondout Lighthouse Collection, Hudson River Maritime Museum, Kingston, New York.*

IX. Catherine A. Murdock at Rondout Creek Light Station, New York, 1857-1907 ᦑ

The first lighthouse at the entrance of Rondout Creek on the west side of the Hudson River was constructed of wood in 1837. George W. Murdock took his wife and two small children to that station in 1856. By then the structure was much damaged by weather and ice. Although it was rickety and not entirely safe, Catherine Murdock was expecting a third child and too busy to worry about her surroundings.

Within a year after his appointment, George Murdock drowned while going ashore to purchase groceries. He was found in the water beside his loaded boat, apparently on his way back to the lighthouse. Despite the tragedy and the attention her young children required, Catherine Murdock continued faithfully to maintain the light.

Others applied for the lightkeeper's position, but local friends praised Catherine Murdock's diligence and recommended her for the post. She received the appointment in 1857. She spent a decade (including the Civil War years) in the old lighthouse, which was threatened repeatedly by severe storms and spring flooding. One storm in particular was so fierce that "the house rocked to and fro like a church steeple." Although Catherine feared the building might collapse, she knew how hazardous the river would be for boatmen without the light to keep them on course. She stayed at her post and kept the light shining in the tower.

In 1867 a new lighthouse (referred to as Rondout I) was constructed of stone on the south side of the creek entrance. The lantern was inside a square granite tower in the northeast angle of the dwelling on a round granite pier. The keeper's house was a solid, cozy structure with four rooms on each of its two floors. A local newspaper described it as "a little waterborne castle." Photographs of the time show the family parlor filled with dark Victorian furniture and the walls hung with framed photographs and prints.

Catherine Murdock lived more than 40 years in her castle. From her island home she witnessed the sinking of the passenger steamboat *Dean Richmond* and the burning of the steamboats *Thorn* and *Clifton* and the barge *Gilboa*. She told a newspaper reporter that the sight of the *Clifton* filled her with awe. It was one mighty mass of flame as it drifted down the Hudson. She and her son rescued several seamen, nursing some back to health. Catherine seldom reported these efforts because she disliked filling out the required forms.

One morning, before dikes were built on each side of the Rondout Creek entrance, Catherine's peaceful sewing was interrupted by a loud crash and the splintering of glass. She turned around and found a schooner's bowsprit sticking through the window and halfway into her room. The schooner had been crowded into the lighthouse by a steam tug towing a line of barges out of Rondout Creek.

The lighthouse was very pleasant in summer, when 20 or 30 visitors a day stopped by to climb the tower. But winters were cold and dreary, punctuated by "heavy and perilous storms." The worst experience that Catherine Murdock recalled was a flood in December of 1878. On the previous day, as a very heavy snowstorm turned into pouring rain, a family friend visiting the lighthouse urged Catherine to go safely ashore. She replied, "I'm a woman, I know, but if the Lighthouse goes down tonight, I go with it."

When she climbed the tower at midnight to replace the lamps, all she could hear in the pitch-dark night was the roar of rushing, rising water. At 3 a.m., the dam at Eddyville upstream on Rondout Creek gave way. The flood carried away houses and barns, tore boats, barges, and tugs from their moorings, and swept everything down the raging current. Catherine could hear crashing noises in the darkness, but the lighthouse stood firm, the light shining brightly in the tower. When daylight revealed her surroundings, the flats were strewn with wrecks and a schooner rested on top of the dike, a live horse trembling beside it.

In 1880 Catherine's son James was appointed assistant keeper. He and his wife lived in the lighthouse with his mother. Catherine Murdock, who had remarried in the interim, retired in 1907 and moved ashore. James succeeded her as official keeper, remaining until 1915. Then Rondout I was replaced with three-story Rondout II, set on a concrete pier.

Rondout I was dismantled in the 1950s. Rondout II light was automated in 1954, and the building leased in 1984 to the Hudson River Maritime Museum.

This chapter is based on articles, correspondence from the Rondout Lighthouse collection at the Hudson River Maritime Museum in Kingston, New York.

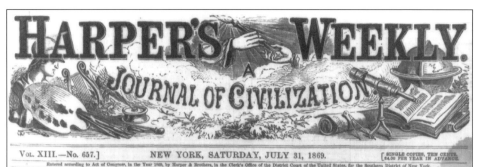

HARPER'S WEEKLY.

A JOURNAL OF CIVILIZATION

VOL. XIII.—No. 657.]   NEW YORK, SATURDAY, JULY 31, 1869.   [SINGLE COPIES, TEN CENTS. / $4.00 PER YEAR IN ADVANCE.

Entered according to Act of Congress, in the Year 1869, by Harper & Brothers, in the Clerk's Office of the District Court of the United States, for the Southern District of New York.

MISS IDA LEWIS, THE HEROINE OF NEWPORT.—Phot. by Manchester Brothers, Providence, R. I.—[See Page 484.]

X. Ida Lewis at Lime Rock Light Station, Rhode Island, 1857-1911 ⏝

Idawalley Zorada Lewis, called Ida, was born in Newport, Rhode Island, in 1842. Her father, Captain Hosea Lewis, was a coast pilot whose health was declining. In 1853 he was appointed the first keeper of nearby Lime Rock beacon on a tiny island a third of a mile from the shore of Newport. At first there was only a temporary lantern and a rough shed that provided shelter for the keeper in bad weather. Lewis's family remained in Newport until 1857. Then a Greek Revival building with a hip roof was constructed on the island. Lewis moved his family into the lighthouse when Ida, the eldest of four children, was 15.

A Newport journalist, George Brewerton, writing a feature story about Ida some years later, described the lighthouse:

> The house itself is a square two-story building, plain even to ugliness, containing a parlor, dining-room and hall, with an L serving as a kitchen below. Above we find three bed-rooms, two large and one small, with a passage way and elevated closet, raised a step or two and reached by a door from the hall, to contain the lamp. Strangers imagine a tower, more or less lofty, . . . and are consequently disappointed . . .. A narrow window, slightly projecting and fitted with glass upon three sides to hold the lamp, is all that the land-locked position of the place requires to fulfill the purpose for which it was erected. . . .

Facing page: *Ida Lewis, famous for her daring rescues at Lime Rock Light Station, was on the cover of* Harper's Weekly *in July 1869. Courtesy of the U.S. Coast Guard.*

Ida Lewis tended the Lime Rock Light Station at Newport Harbor, Rhode Island, from 1857 to 1911. The station now serves as a yacht club. Courtesy of the U.S. Coast Guard.

Hosea Lewis had been at Lime Rock less than four months when he was disabled by a stroke. Like many wives and daughters of lighthouse keepers before and after, Ida expanded her domestic duties. To the care of her invalid father and a seriously ill sister was added the care of the light. All these responsibilities made it impossible for Ida to attend school.

Since Lime Rock was completely surrounded by water, the only way to reach the mainland was by boat. In the mid-19th century most women didn't row boats. Ida rowed her siblings to school every weekday and fetched needed supplies from the town. The wooden boat was heavy, but she became very skillful in handling it. Ida was also reputed to be the best swimmer in all Newport.

In a newspaper clipping of the time, her father is quoted as saying,

> Again and again I have seen the children from this window as they were returning from school in some heavy blow, when Ida alone was with them, and old sailor that I am, I felt that I would not give a penny for their lives, so furious was the storm. . . . I have watched them till I could not bear to look any longer, expecting any moment to see

them swamped, . . . and then I have turned away and said to my wife, let me know if they get safe in, for I could not endure to see them perish and realize that we were powerless to save them.

Ida's skill at the oars was regularly tested. During her first year at Lime Rock, four young men who were out sailing nearly drowned. One of them had foolishly shimmied up the mast and rocked the boat to tease his companions. The boat capsized. Four boys who couldn't swim clung to the overturned hull, shouting for help.

Ida heard them and rowed to their rescue. In their terror, they almost dragged her overboard, but she pulled all four over the stern into her boat and returned them to land. This was only the first of a number of rescues that made Ida famous.

Ida Lewis, keeper of Lime Rock Lighthouse, extends a gaff to a floundering victim while her younger brother Rudolph steadies the boat with his oars. In the background is Lime Rock Lighthouse. Courtesy of the artist, John Witt.

Ida and her mother tended the Lime Rock Light for her father from 1857 until 1872, when he died. Her mother was appointed keeper until 1879, although Ida continued to do the keeper's work. Then Ida received the official appointment and her own salary ($500 a year).

Because of her many rescues, Ida Lewis became the best-known lighthouse keeper of her day. During her 54 years on Lime Rock, she is credited with saving 18 lives. Unofficial reports suggest the number may have been as high as 25. One such rescue, on March 29, 1869, is immortalized in a painting by John Witt, commissioned by the U.S. Coast Guard.

Ida's fame spread quickly after the 1869 rescue, for a reporter was sent from the *New York Tribune* to record her deeds. Articles also appeared in *Harper's Weekly, Leslie's* magazine, and other leading newspapers. The Life Saving Benevolent Association of New York sent her a silver medal and a check for $100—a substantial sum to a young woman who then earned $600 a year.

A parade was held in Ida's honor in Newport on Independence Day. Officials presented Ida with a sleek mahogany rowboat with red velvet cushions, gold braid around the gunwales, and gold-plated oarlocks. When she was 64, Ida became a life beneficiary of the Carnegie Hero Fund, receiving a monthly pension of $30.

Tales of Ida Lewis's skill and courage spread so widely that both President Ulysses S. Grant and Vice President Schuyler Colfax came to visit her in 1869. Colfax went out to the lighthouse to meet her, but there are two versions of Ida's meeting with President Grant. One says that as Grant landed on Lime Rock, he stepped into water and got his feet wet. "I have come to see Ida Lewis," he remarked, "and to see her I'd get wet up to my armpits if necessary." The other version states that Ida rowed to shore and was conducted to the President's carriage to meet him and his wife.

Fame brought countless other visitors to the island to stare at Ida. Her wheelchair-bound father entertained himself by counting their numbers—often a hundred a day. Nine thousand came in one summer. Ida also received numerous

Ida Lewis performed the duties of keeper at Lime Rock Light for her father beginning in 1857; however, she did not receive the official appointment until 1879. Courtesy of the National Archives, #26-LG-69-60.

gifts, letters, and even proposals of marriage. She disliked all the attention.

In 1881 the *Annual Report of the U.S. Life-Saving Service* reported that the highest medal awarded by the Life-Saving Service had been presented to Ida Lewis for saving thirteen persons from drowning.

Ida's last recorded rescue occurred when she was 63 years old. A close friend, rowing out to the lighthouse, stood up in her boat, lost her balance and fell overboard. Ida launched a lifeboat and hauled the woman aboard. When asked where she found her strength and courage, she replied, "I don't know, I ain't particularly strong. The Lord Almighty gives it to me when I need it, that's all."

Ida continued at her post until her own death in 1911. On the night she died, the bells on all the vessels anchored in Newport Harbor were tolled in her honor.

In 1924 the Rhode Island legislature officially changed the name of Lime Rock to Ida Lewis Rock. This allowed the Lighthouse Service to change the name of the Lime Rock Lighthouse to the Ida Lewis Rock Lighthouse—the only such honor ever paid to a keeper. Later the Newport Yacht Club bought the lighthouse and put a light back in the old lantern as a private aid to navigation.

In 1995 the Coast Guard launched the first of a series of new keeper-class buoy tenders and named it *Ida Lewis*. In addition to her aids to navigation (ATON) duties, USCGC *Ida Lewis* tends the grave of Ida Lewis and assists in port security in and around New York Harbor.

Sources for this chapter include an entry on Ida Lewis in Notable American Women *(Harvard University Press, 1971); Dennis L. Noble, "Historical Paintings Project: Ida Lewis, Keeper of Lime Rock Lighthouse and the Rescue of Two Men on 4 February 1881," Coast Guard monograph; clippings filed in the Coast Guard Historian's Office in Washington, D.C.; and U.S. Department of Transportation* News, *CG 34-95.*

XI. Harriet Colfax at Michigan City Light Station, Indiana, 1861-1904 ᠵ

The short coast of the state of Indiana along Lake Michigan has one historic light that guided Great Lakes mariners for more than a century. Its history began in 1835, when the founder of Michigan City deeded to the United States government a tract of shore property on which to build a lighthouse.

The first light was hung on a tall post located slightly west of the present lighthouse. The first lighthouse, built in 1837, had a 40-foot-high whitewashed tower topped with a lantern to house the light.

As the shipping of grain and lumber increased, a brighter light was needed. In 1858 a new lighthouse was built, with a tower and lantern on the north end. Its fixed light with a Fresnel lens of the fifth order was visible for 15 miles.

In the 19th century many keepers were political appointees. Harriet Colfax's appointment as keeper in 1861 may have been arranged by her cousin, Schuyler Colfax, then a member of Congress.

Harriet was 37 when she took up her duties at an initial salary of $350 a year. Critics thought her too small and fragile for the job, but Harriet performed her duties without fail for 43 years.

Piers guarded both sides of the entrance to Michigan City Harbor. In 1871 a beacon light and elevated walk were installed on the east pier, which extended 1,500 feet into Lake Michigan. The keeper of the shore light maintained this light as well.

A year later all keepers were required to keep journals. Harriet Colfax's log is in the National Archives. Her crisp record of her daily activities gives a very vivid picture of her life at the Michigan City Light.

> August 12, 1872. *Clear & Warm, with light E. Winds. U.S. Tender* Haze *came in about 5 a.m. with supplies for the St[ation] House. Commodore Murray, Lt. House Inspector, called at the Lt. House. Expressed himself satisfied with everything about the establishment.*

> August 16, 1872. *This is the day on which the Comet was to strike the Earth and demolish all things terrestrial—but failed to come up to appointment. The elevated walk [on the east pier] was run into by a Vessel entering the harbor & considerably damaged. 5 [ship] arrivals.*

Harriet Colfax reported damage to the elevated walkway several times a year. This walkway was a wooden structure raised above the pier on metal struts, allowing the keeper to reach the beacon on the end of the pier when storms swept water over the pier. Many moments of real danger were associated with that walkway.

> September 18, 1872. *Cold day. Heavy N. W. gale towards night. The waves dashing over both Piers, very nearly carrying me with them into the lake.*

Imagine her walking along the elevated walkway. Harriet Colfax probably did not wear trousers, nor did she have yellow slickers to keep her dry. She may have worn an oilskin coat over her long dress, but her heavy skirts must have dragged around her ankles as they got wet. Freezing weather made the footing slippery. In cold weather the lard oil to fuel the lamp for the beacon had to be heated to keep it from solidifying. If she was delayed waiting for high waves to pass and too much time elapsed in reaching the beacon, the oil congealed and would not ignite. Then she had to return to the station house and reheat it. The storms she described buffeted her with wild gusts of wind, flinging not only waves across the walkway, but also blinding sheets of spray and sleet. When her task was finally completed, her soaked clothes would have been hung to dry by the wood stove. She had no hot shower to revive her.

Barely ten days later, September 29. *Wind blowing a westerly gale all day & still rising at 5 p.m. Four vessels entered while the gale was at its height & ran against the elevated walk, breaking it in again. Went to the beacon tonight with considerable risk of life.*

The next day Harriet mentioned that "the sails of the vessels which entered in yesterday's storm were hanging in shreds, but no other injuries sustained." A month later in another storm, a vessel went ashore east of the piers. The next day's entry: *The Sch[ooner]* Scotland *went to pieces and sank in the night. Gathered the particulars of the wreck & reported the same to Com. Murray at Detroit—Lt. H. Inspector. The Gale of yesterday continued unabated. 1arrival.*

Storms pounded Lake Michigan as winter set in. November 19, 1872. *Terrible day. Wind blowing a northerly*

A 1914 view of Michigan City Light Station at Michigan City, Indiana, kept by Harriet Colfax from 1861 until 1904. After the light was automated in the 1960s, the City of Michigan City purchased the keeper's house and established a museum in it. Courtesy of the National Archives, #26-LG-56-30.

A later pier at Michigan City Light in rough weather. The light keeper walked out on this type of elevated walkway to light the beacon at the end. Courtesy of the National Archives, #26-LG-56-32.

gale—snowing & drifting. Crossing good on the ice [of the frozen harbor]. Looks as tho' Winter was fairly upon us, & a few days at the farthest would close up navigation. The City of Tawas *has made her last trip & will go into Winter quarters here. Other vessels reported in Chicago papers following suit—also a good many wrecks, with fearful loss of life.*

Finally, on December 13, Harriet *Put the lamps, etc. away for the Winter, covered from dust & dampness.* This end-of-season ritual included cleaning and polishing the lamps and wrapping up the lens in cotton batting and kerosene. All the parts were stored in the oil house. Then Harriet washed the glass and painted all the wood surfaces in the lantern.

During the months when the harbor was closed, Harriet recorded only the weather. Shipping resumed the following May.

Summer weather made her post more attractive: her entries mention "large numbers of visitors [coming from the town] to see the lamps." Ships entering the harbor brought visitors as well.

August 17, 1873. *The Supply Vessel* Haze *put in (as usual) a very unexpected appearance this morning about 7 o'clock. Commodore Murray, L. H. Inspector, Captain Davis of the L. H. Board & Col. Wilkins, U.S.A., were aboard & came up to the house. The Officers expressed themselves much pleased with the buildings, lanterns, light, apparatus, etc.*

But as fall arrived, Harriet was having so much trouble getting to the beacon that on October 20 she petitioned the Light-House Board to give her an assistant to tend the beacon. Her request was granted. November 23. *The man in temporary charge of the Beacon Light was unable to reach it tonight— consequently the Light was not exhibited. Storm increasing in fury when the Sun went down.*

The next day part of the elevated walkway was carried away and the beacon again went unlighted.

Harriet recorded wild, damaging storms every year. December 5, 1885. *Gale continues, with snow—cold. Elevated walk badly damaged & beacon light damaged and put out. The beacon cannot be repaired this fall.*

The next night the beacon was carried away in the storm. The following two nights Harriet sent a man in a tug to hang a lantern. The next day she asked permission to use the tug the rest of the season. In March the inspector made her re-explain the causes of the darkened beacon and the need for a tug to light it.

In March of 1886 a storm carried away the entire superstructure on the west pier. The beacon was not replaced by a temporary light until June. In October the temporary light and the beacon structure were both swept away and thrown up onto the beach.

Every month Harriet mentioned preparing a monthly report, four times a year a quarterly report, and every winter an annual report to send to the Light-House Board. She recorded various leaves of absence once she had an assistant to care for the station. In 1876 she visited the Centennial Exposition in Philadelphia. In the summer she visited friends for two weeks, and also spent the Christmas holidays away. In 1887 she requested leave throughout the entire winter when the lights were closed.

Many of her entries related to the domestic tasks involved in keeping the light. In May of 1879 she noted that she had sewn rings on lantern curtains for the beacon. The curtains were hung around the lens in the daytime to protect it from dust and sunlight. Repeated entries mention cleaning and polishing the prisms and shining the brass.

Other notations give glimpses of life in the station house. She wrote almost every year of painting the stairs and floors and having the station house and the oil house painted. (Normally keepers were required to do all such painting, but women were exempted from painting whole buildings.)

Twice Harriet wrote that soot in the wood stove chimney caught fire, "causing quite a fright." Each fall she received a check ($20 to $30) for wood to heat her house. The Light-House Board continued to pay for wood until 1882, when they informed Harriet that she would have to pay for her own thereafter.

This sounds petty, but the keeper's small salary was augmented by free housing, and some received rations (delivered periodically by lighthouse tender). In 1882 the allowance for isolated keepers included 200 pounds of pork, 100 pounds of beef, 50 pounds of sugar, 2 barrels of flour, 24 pounds of coffee, 10 gallons of beans, 4 gallons of vinegar, 2 barrels of potatoes, 50 pounds of rice, and 13 ounces of mustard and pepper. (This probably did not apply to Harriet.)

One tantalizing entry refers to repairs to the 'water closet', and then to having the outside of the water closet (outhouse) and lattices painted.

Harriet wrote of seeing a mirage from the lantern, of a total eclipse of the moon, of a double rainbow, of hailstorms, of glorious displays of Northern Lights. She recorded the day President Garfield was shot and the deaths of President Grant and Vice President Hendricks in 1885. She mentions an order from the Light-House Board outlining the official uniform she was supposed to wear (double-breasted coat with yellow buttons, dark blue trousers, and a cap bearing a yellow metal

Harriet Colfax, keeper of the Michigan City Light Station in Michigan City, Indiana, from 1861 until 1904. Courtesy of the Old Lighthouse Museum, Michigan City Historical Society, Inc.

lighthouse badge). The inspector assured her that "women keepers were exempted" from this order.

Local deaths were recorded—the drowning of three fishermen after their boat capsized, a schooner captain struck by an engine, another drowned ten miles away from Michigan City Lighthouse. In 1885 the lighthouse keeper at Racine, Wisconsin, drowned in a storm. In 1886 a barge mate in her own harbor was struck in the head by a heavy log and killed.

Harriet received and acknowledged shipments of oil, wick, lamps, and other supplies. In 1882 instructions from the District Lighthouse Engineer told her to clean the lard oil lamps in preparation for exchanging them for kerosene (known as mineral oil) lamps. Occasionally she was asked to ship surplus oil to a neighboring light station.

One of the most surprising requests to come from the inspector was an instruction to "find out all about the birds and insects in this vicinity." Harriet felt that this was beyond her depth, so she "turned the letter over to the resident taxidurmist [*sic*]." A follow-up inquiry asked about bird migrations.

The Light-House Board's finances must have been tight in 1882, for the assistant's position at the Michigan City Light was revoked. Harriet, then 58 years old, wrote letters all winter asking for help in tending the beacon. She kept both lights by herself through the following summer, and finally received permission in September to reemploy her former assistant.

In 1888 the Light-House Board reduced Harriet's salary from $600 annually to $540. No explanation was given, nor did Harriet record any dismay.

Several annual reports in the 1890s recommended the addition of a fog signal to the station. Its construction was undertaken in 1904, and coincided with Harriet's retirement.

> October 6, 1904. *Commenced taking inventory of public property. October 8. Sold household effects preparatory to vacating dear old St. House. October 11. The new Keeper arrived today and made pleasant call at St. House.*

Harriet's last entry in the official log was on October 12. She retired at age 80 because of failing health. She died a year later.

⋆⇒◯⇐⋆

Sources for this chapter include Harriet Colfax's log in the National Archives, Record Group 26, Washington, D.C.; information sheets from the Old Lighthouse Museum, Michigan City Historical Society; Patricia Harris, "Michigan City: Indiana's Only Lighthouse" in The Keeper's Log, *spring 1987; Susan Meyer, "A woman's place was in the lighthouse" in* USCG Commandant's Bulletin 47-80.

XII. Mary Ryan at Calumet Harbor Entrance Light Station, Indiana, 1873-1880 ᗡ

A lighthouse keeper without a family had to deal with solitude. Not all women keepers were happy in their assignments. Mary Ryan kept the Calumet Harbor Entrance Light in Indiana (located offshore on a pier) from 1873 to 1880 after her husband died. Her log reveals the hardships of her post.

December 25, 1873. *I was suppose[d] to have been informed when this light would be discontinued [for the winter], not a vessel since the 15th of Nov. and nothing to light for and this is such a dreary place to be in all alone.*

April 7, 1874. *Oh, for a home in the sunny south, such a climate.*

April 16. *Such a time, everyone is despaired thinking that summer is never coming.*

May 1. *So cold, Mayday!, those people who go for flowers will be disappointed.*

May 2. *Nothing but gloom, without and WITHIN.*

October 31. *A promise of a cold hard winter as the signs show, so many out of employment this early in the season, and what will it be before winter is over? God "only knows."*

April 22, 1880. *I think some changes will have to be made, this is not a fit place for anyone to live in.*

July 31. *This has been the most trying month of my keeping a lighthouse, the most important question, can anything worse come?*

August 28. *The lighthouse engineers never do anything for me.*

August 30. *Oh what a place.*

November 1. *This is all gloom and darkness.*

Calumet Harbor Light Station on Lake Michigan just east of Chicago in 1914. Courtesy of the National Archives, #26-LG-55-13.

Mary Ryan was doubtless very pleased when her replacement arrived late in 1880.

⊷⟞⟝⊶

This chapter is based on Mary Ryan's log entries, published in The Keeper's Log, *spring 1991.*

XIII. Julia Williams, 1865-1905, and Caroline Morse, 1905-1911, at Santa Barbara Light Station, California ᣠ

The discovery of gold in California in 1848 led to the rapid growth of ports on the Pacific coast. The Santa Barbara Channel was particularly hazardous for early mariners. Many ships were wrecked before the Santa Barbara lighthouse was erected in 1856.

Johnson Williams, originally from Kennebec, Maine, took his family to California in 1850. In 1856 they traveled by horse and oxcart to Santa Barbara to occupy the barely completed lighthouse (built in the uniform cottage style popular at the time). Not even a road led from the town to the mesa on which it stood.

Santa Barbara was so small in those days that Julia Williams could invite all 30 Americans in the town to a Christmas dinner at the lighthouse in 1857. This would have been a major social occasion for women whose contacts with other women and their families were limited by distance and meager transport.

A Williams baby was born in the lighthouse two months before the three lamps were first displayed in the lantern. In 1904 this child, named Bion, wrote an entertaining account of those early days, entitled "The Santa Barbara Light and its Keeper."

The isolation of the lighthouse during Bion's childhood provided many challenges. His father had another job in town, leaving his mother very much on her own. Women who went west in the mid-19th century performed a multitude of domestic tasks. Fresh water was to be caught in a cistern, but rain seldom fell. Julia saddled a horse, took the baby in her arms, and, followed by two little girls, rode a mile to a spring to bring home cans of water slung to the saddle. She gathered wood for her cook stove in the same manner. She did her own sewing and mending.

Many years later her grandson, True Maxfield, remembered particularly the excellent fresh-baked bread his grandmother gave him, and the masses of orange and yellow nasturtiums blooming in the lighthouse yard.

In the early days all supplies came to the few stores in nearby Santa Barbara in small sailing vessels, arriving every month or two. When something ran out, customers waited for the next ship. Without even a right-of-way to the lighthouse until 1877, getting to town to fetch supplies was a challenge in itself. Mission Creek ran between the lighthouse and the town and had to be waded. On those rare occasions when rain flooded the creek, the crossing was perilous.

Santa Barbara Light Station in California was first lighted in 1856. Julia Williams was keeper from 1865 to 1905; Caroline Morse from 1905 to 1911. The lighthouse was demolished in the 1925 earthquake. Courtesy of the U.S. Coast Guard.

Julia Williams, keeper of the Santa Barbara Light Station, California, 1865-1905. Courtesy of the Santa Barbara Historical Society.

By 1860 Mr. Williams had purchased a ranch nearby and lost interest in the lighthouse. He sent his hired man every night to light the lamp. In 1865 his wife Julia agreed to tend the light at a salary of $750 a year. She had produced another baby in the interim, and bore two more in 1866 and 1869. Mr. Williams continued ranching until his death in 1882. The Williams's son Frank grew corn and beans on the surrounding land and became a prosperous farmer. His brother Albert grazed dairy cows.

Julia Williams stayed at her post until 1905, when she was 80 years old. In 1911 a local newspaper printed the following obituary:

> Mrs. Julia F. Williams, who for forty years was keeper of the Santa Barbara lighthouse, died Friday night at the Cottage hospital where she had been a patient sufferer since her fall [which broke her hip] at the lighthouse six years ago.
>
> "The Lighthouse Lady," a title won by years of faithful service, was known to every naval officer and coasting captain that crossed the Channel. She was identified with the pioneer history of this city, being the first American woman in the presidio of Santa Barbara, and her memory was a veritable mine of early events. Her life of faithful service made hers one of the most historic and picturesque careers of the Pacific coast. . . .
>
> In the forty years of service she was never out of sight of the house after dark. Every night she climbed the three flights of stairs at sunset and lighted the lamp. Every night at midnight the lamp was trimmed or changed for a fresh one, and every morning as the sun touched the mountain tops the same hand extinguished the light and drew the curtain across the lens and went about her household duties.

Julia Williams was succeeded at the Santa Barbara Light Station by Caroline Morse, who was keeper from 1905 to 1911. The lighthouse was demolished in the earthquake of 1925 and replaced with an acetylene-powered light on a wooden tower.

The Santa Barbara Historical Society provided newspaper clippings and Bion Williams's memoir for this chapter; and Ross Holland of the National Park Service interviewed her grandson, True Maxfield.

XIV. Mary Terry at Sand Point Light Station, Michigan, 1868-1886 ᕽ

Mary Terry's husband John was appointed the first keeper of the new lighthouse on Sand Point at Escanaba, Michigan, while it was still under construction in 1867. John died of tuberculosis before the lighthouse was completed. The citizens of Escanaba recommended that his wife replace him. Local government officials strongly opposed the idea, but Mary received the official appointment in 1868 and began the operation of the new light.

She apparently met the challenge. The Escanaba *Iron Port* reported that "she was a very methodical woman, very careful in the discharge of her duties and very particular in the care of the property under her charge." Mary Terry maintained the light on Lake Michigan's cold and windy northern shore for almost 18 years, using a wood furnace to keep warm in winter.

In March of 1886 the handyman who helped Mary with maintenance noticed that the wood near the furnace was hot. When he called the keeper's attention to it, she replied that she expected to be burned out one day, but added that she slept with one eye open.

The following night fire destroyed the lighthouse. When the alarm was given, at about one o'clock, the flames had enveloped the building and broken through the roof; nothing could be saved and Mary was missing..

The Deputy Collector in Escanaba wrote on March 5 to the Light-House Board:

> . . . saddest of all was the remains of Mrs. Capt. Terry was found in the ruins; deeming it my duty to thus inform

you of this event, Mrs. Terry being Keeper of said Light House. . . .

Those who knew Mary Terry had difficulty believing that someone so efficient could have died by accident or her own carelessness. Her body was found in the oilroom in the southwest corner of the lighthouse, and not in her bedroom. This led some to think that she was the victim of murder, robbery, and arson. At age 69 she was reputed to be a woman of means, who had several thousand dollars in a savings account and had purchased several valuable building lots in the city.

The verdict of the coroner's jury a week later "that Mrs. Terry came to her death from causes and by means to the jury unknown was," according to the March 13 issue of the *Iron Port*,

> . . . the only one that could be rendered. There was and is a general feeling of suspicion, based on Mrs. Terry's known cool headedness, that she did not come to her end accidentally, and this feeling is strengthened by the fact that the south door was found open and that the lock was found with the bolt shot forward as though the door had been forced, not unlocked, but the theory of robbery does not find support in the fact that money, gold pieces, were found where they would have fallen from the cupboard, the place where she usually kept what she kept in the house, and that a bundle of papers, insurance policy, deeds, etc., charred throughout but preserving its form sufficiently to show what it had been, was also found.
>
> The verdict, then, was the only one possible, and the truth of the affair can never be known. There may have been foul play, but there is no evidence to justify an assertion that there was; no circumstances that are not consistent with a theory of accidental death.

Sources for this chapter include Richard Stratton, "Two Women among Nine Sand Point Lighthouse Keepers" in The Delta Historian; *newspaper clippings supplied by the Delta County Historical Society; National Archives Record Group 26, Entry 36.*

Mary Terry kept the Sand Point Light Station at Escanaba, Michigan, from 1868 to 1886, when she died in a fire that destroyed the lighthouse. This photo was part of a stereoscopic view by George W. Bauder from the Robert N. Dennis Collection of Stereoscopic Views, Miriam & Ira Division of Art, Prints & Photographs, The New York Public Library, Astor, Lenox and Tilden Foundations.

Stony Point Light Station on the Hudson River, kept by Nancy Rose from 1871 until 1904. The 1826 tower is now in a state park. Courtesy of the National Archives, #26-LG-17-1.

XV. Nancy Rose, 1871-1904, and Melinda Rose, 1904-1905, at Stony Point Light Station, New York ๛

Our picture of Mrs. Nancy Rose comes from an article published in the *New York Tribune* on June 28, 1903, shortly before she was to retire. Nancy intended to move from the lighthouse high above the Hudson River on the crest of Stony Point to a cottage being built in the village at the base of the mountain.

Nancy Rose's uncle, appointed in 1825, had been the first keeper at Stony Point. Nancy's husband, Alexander Rose, became the second keeper in the spring of 1852. Two decades later, while carrying timbers for the bell tower that the government was then constructing, he ruptured a blood vessel and died a few weeks later. After his death his wife took over his duties, trimming the lights and keeping the fogbell going from one end of the year to the next. The Hudson River is often open to navigation throughout the winter. Nancy Rose lived in the little six-room cottage on the heights for 50 years. She was official keeper for 33 of those years, with sole responsibility for two beacon lights and a fogbell.

The lighthouse on Stony Point was built in 1826 within Stony Point Fort. The old fort walls had been filled in to become a terrace of grass and shrubs. The Rose family frequently found bullets and grapeshot, rusty and soil-eaten, around the fort. A flagpole marked the spot where Mad Anthony Wayne, of Revolutionary War fame, was supposed to have fallen. Nancy Rose's great-grandfather, Jacob Parkinson, was wounded in the same battle.

From the little balcony around the lantern one could see for miles up and down the Hudson River. The rolling hills followed its course, blue and misty as they melted away to the horizon. The trim little cottage on the mountain top was surrounded with climbing roses and old-fashioned shrubs. Nancy Rose kept the interior immaculate.

In bad weather the fog machinery had to be wound up every three and three-quarters hours. The lighthouse lamps were replenished with oil every midnight. In 1880 the fogbell was moved from the light station at the top of the hill to a spot nearer the water. This required the keeper to hike back and forth to the site whenever fog closed in. In 1902 a red lens lantern was placed on top of the belltower near the water, again increasing the keeper's duties. It had to be trimmed and tended nightly. Nancy Rose's salary remained the same throughout, however—$500 a year.

Nancy never left the station without notifying the inspector of her intended absence. She recorded weather conditions every day, along with the time of lighting and extinguishing the lamps, and the disposal of every ounce of supplies and inch of wick. The lighthouse inspector came unheralded in his tender at uncertain intervals. He brought supplies and inspected the 500 aids to navigation in his district. He went over the entire premises, even the garret, cellar, and barn. No criticism of Nancy Rose's lighthouse was ever recorded.

The *Tribune* reporter who interviewed Nancy when she was 79 years old also found everything about Stony Point Light "exquisitely clean. A new coat of gray paint has just made the woodwork resplendent, and the copper floor of the light chamber is burnished like gold. There is even a great canvas hood, with which the huge refracting lenses are covered during the day to keep any speck of dust from the polished metal and glass."

Only two of Nancy's six children survived—Melinda and Alexander—both of whom lived with their mother. Boredom seems to have played some part in the family's decision to leave the lighthouse. "You must have had many interesting experiences?" Nancy was asked by the reporter.

"No," was the answer. "Nothing ever happens up here. One year is exactly like another, and except for the weather, nothing changes."

Melinda's reaction was much the same.

> I can't remember anything that has ever happened, except once our cow died, and several times it's been bad years for the chickens. But even the one wreck wasn't really what you might call a wreck, for nobody was hurt, and it wasn't mother's fault anyhow, for both the lights were burning as brightly as ever.

The wreck that was the highlight of their sojourn at Stony Point occurred in 1901, between 1 and 2 a.m. on a windy, rainy March morning. *Poughkeepsie*, a Central Hudson Steamboat Company passenger ship, went aground. Nancy Rose had just returned from her nightly visit to the light and was changing her storm-soaked clothes when a pounding on her door startled her. Outside forty or fifty persons, among them seven women, sought shelter from the storm. The Roses did what they could, building a roaring fire in the kitchen stove to dry shoes and garments and dispensing hot coffee until the next train to New York was due.

The Roses' disenchantment with the lighthouse may have increased when a state park was placed on Stony Point. After it opened, the lighthouse grounds were overrun in summer months with picnickers and sightseers who wanted to tour the whole place, including the tower.

Official instructions about visitors at light stations were very specific:

> Keepers must be courteous and polite to all visitors and show them everything of interest about the station at such times as will not interfere with light-house duties. Keepers must not allow visitors to handle the apparatus or deface light-house property. Special care must be taken to prevent the scratching of names or initials on the glass of the lanterns or on the windows of the towers. The keeper on duty at the time is responsible for any injury or defacement to the buildings, lenses, lamps, glazing of the lantern and to any other light-house property under his charge, . . . No visitor should be admitted to the tower

unless attended by a keeper, nor in the watch room or lantern between sunset and sunrise.

The lantern in the Stony Point Light was reached by three sets of steep steps, with locked doors and trapdoors. The Roses probably found the repeated climbing of the stairs and the supervision of large numbers of park visitors trying.

Nancy Rose apparently never left the lighthouse to live in her new house, for she died in 1904. Her daughter Melinda could not have been completely disenchanted with the Stony Point Station, for she applied to succeed her mother as keeper. Lighthouse keepers had been moved into the Civil Service in 1896. When told that she was too old (53) to qualify under the new rules, Melinda sought the help of her congressman. He had the age requirement waived so she could take the examination and establish her eligibility. She had been assisting her mother for years, and received at least two temporary appointments. Her official appointment is recorded in 1904. In 1905 she submitted her resignation with the following comment: "I find the care and responsibility too great for one keeper to attend to two lights and one fog signal for the sum of $560 per annum." She also mentioned the loneliness of Stony Point in the winter. Melinda was succeeded by a male keeper.

Stony Point Battlefield personnel provided clippings and a short memoir by Melinda Rose. Other sources include 1902 Instructions to Light-Keepers; *and* The World, *November 20, 1905.*

XVI. Elizabeth Williams at Beaver Island Harbor Point Light Station, Michigan, 1872-1884, and at Little Traverse Light Station, Michigan, 1884-1913 ༄

Elizabeth Whitney, born on Mackinac Island, Michigan, in 1842, grew up on Beaver Island in Northern Lake Michigan. In 1869, some years after she married Clement Van Riper, he was appointed keeper of the Harbor Point Light Station on the northeast side of Beaver Island.

Elizabeth was unusual in the ranks of women keepers in that she spent many of her solitary hours writing. Much of her book, *A Child of the Sea; and Life among the Mormons,* deals with her childhood spent near a Mormon settlement on Beaver Island, but the last 20 pages detail her life in two lighthouses on Lake Michigan.

In the spring of 1870 a large force of men came with material to build a new tower and repair the dwelling, adding a new brick kitchen. A new fourth order lens was placed in the new tower and the color of the light changed from white to red. These improvements were a great addition to the station from what it had been. My husband having now very poor health, I took charge of the care of the lamps, and the beautiful lens in the tower was my especial care. On stormy nights I watched the light that no accident might happen. We burned the lard oil, which needed great care, especially in cold weather, when the oil would congeal and fail to flow fast enough to the wicks. In long nights the lamps had to be trimmed twice each night, and sometimes oftener.

Then in 1872 tragedy struck.

One dark and stormy night we heard the flapping of sails and saw the lights flashing in the darkness. The ship was in distress. After a hard struggle she reached the harbor and was leaking so badly she sank. My husband in his efforts to assist them lost his life. He was drowned with a companion, the first mate of the schooner *Thomas Howland*. The bodies were never recovered.

In a letter that Elizabeth wrote to the chairman of the Light-House Board on November 15, 1872, she describes how her husband went to "procure the assistance . . . for a schooner which was badly leaking. He went in the company of the first mate of the vessel for he could not get anyone else to go with him . . .. Their boat was found that afternoon near Cross Valley badly broken to pieces . . ... My husband lost his life in trying to aid . . . sailors who were in trouble."

In her book she continued the story:

Life then seemed darker than the midnight storm that raged for three days upon the deep dark waters. I was

Beaver Island Harbor Point Light Station at the north end of Lake Michigan, kept by Elizabeth Whitney Williams from 1872 to 1884. Only the tower currently remains standing. Courtesy of the National Archives, #26-LG-55-7A.

Elizabeth Williams kept two lights on Lake Michigan. Courtesy of Beaver Island Historical Society.

weak from sorrow, but realized that though the life that was dearest to me had gone, yet there were others out in the dark and treacherous waters who needed the rays from the shining light of my tower. Nothing could rouse me but that thought, then all my life and energy was given to the work which now seemed was given me to do.

The light-house was the only home I had and I was glad and willing to do my best in the service. My appointment came in a few weeks after, and since that time I have tried faithfully to perform my duty as a light keeper. At first I felt almost afraid to assume so great a responsibility, knowing it all required watchful care and strength, and many sleepless nights. I now felt a deeper interest in our sailors' lives than ever before, and I longed to do something for humanity's sake, as well as earn my living, having an aged mother dependent upon me for a home.

Although her first husband, two brothers, and three nephews died at sea, Elizabeth's own words make it clear that she loved her work:

I loved the water, having always been near it, and I loved to stand in the tower and watch the great rolling waves chasing and tumbling in upon the shore. It was hard to tell when it was loveliest. Whether in its quiet moods or in a raging foam.

Elizabeth kept the Beaver Island Harbor Point Light Station for 12 years. In 1875 she wrote the Light-House Superintendent as follows:

> I expect to be married sometime in September, and will it make any difference about me keeping the light? Those wise people here say of course I cannot have the light if I marry, but I really don't see why I could not keep as good a light then as now. I have kept it almost 3 years alone and I believe that I have the name among Mariners of keeping one of the best Lights on the Lakes. . ..

Elizabeth continued her duties after her marriage in 1875 to Daniel Williams. In 1884 she requested a transfer to the new lighthouse on Little Traverse Bay, where she remained for 29 years and wrote her book. She gave few details of her career at Little Traverse Light.

In 1900 the lighthouse inspector wrote to the Light-House Board as follows:

> I respectfully recommend that the salary of Mrs. Daniel Williams, keeper of the light station at Little Traverse, Michigan, be increased from $500 to $560 per annum, to date from May 1, 1900.
>
> As this station has now a fog-bell and no assistant keeper, the salary recommended will be in keeping with that of similarly equipped stations in this district.

The salary increase was authorized on May 9, 1900.

This chapter is based on Elizabeth Williams, A Child of the Sea *(privately printed 1905; reprinted by the Beaver Island Historical Society, 1983 and 2004); National Archives Record Group 26, Entries 36 and 24; and* Annual Reports of the Light-House Board.

XVII. Mary Smith at Ediz Hook Light Station, Washington, 1870-1874, and Point Fermin Light Station, 1874-1882; Thelma Austin at Point Fermin Light Station, California, 1925-1941 ᔆ

Increased shipping into San Pedro Harbor led to the construction of a redwood-and-fir Victorian lighthouse on Point Fermin at the harbor entrance in 1874. The building design was identical to that of several other lighthouses erected in California at that time. Two large cisterns and the necessary outbuildings were included, with the entire station enclosed by a substantial fence. The lantern panes and the fourth-order Fresnel lens were shipped from France by way of Cape Horn. Lard oil was the first fuel, then kerosene, followed by electricity in 1925.

The first keepers were sisters, Mary and Helen Smith, although only Mary is named as official keeper. Mary Smith had been keeper at Ediz Hook in Washington Territory from 1870 to 1874, replacing her father George Smith when he resigned. It is possible that Mary's brother Victor Smith, who held the post of Special Treasury Agent, arranged his father's appointment as keeper at Ediz Hook, as well as assistant appointments for his sisters. He may also have arranged Mary's appointment as keeper at Point Fermin. She was paid $800 annually, and her sister received $600 as assistant keeper.

The sisters remained at Point Fermin Light Station until 1882. The salary of the subsequent assistant was reduced, and later the position was abolished.

Mary Smith was keeper of Ediz Hook Light (above), Washington Territory, before receiving a transfer to the new Point Fermin Light Station (below) in California. Courtesy of the U.S. Coast Guard.

The last keeper at Point Fermin was also a woman. Thelma Austin had gone to Point Fermin in 1917 with her family, when her father was appointed keeper. When both parents died in 1925, Thelma, the eldest daughter, took charge of both the lighthouse and her brothers and sisters. Electrification of the light that year ended the routine of cleaning, polishing, and lighting lamps every evening and extinguishing them every morning. Thelma's duties were reduced to the flicking of a switch, and she was able to supplement her keeper's salary by working as a dental assistant in the daytime.

Thelma operated the light until two days before Pearl Harbor, when it was "blacked out." During World War II the lantern room was removed and replaced by a radar lookout. An automated light was established nearby after the war, leading the Coast Guard to turn the building over to a private preservation group. It has been restored to its earlier appearance and is today the popular centerpiece of a city park.

→⇒◯⊂⇐←

Sources for this chapter include Sandra Clunies, "1874-1882 Archives & Anecdotes; 1893 Vintage Photos: Point Fermin Lighthouse," prepared for the Harbor Lights Collectors Society, April 24, 1999; and Lenore Nicholson, "Point Fermin Lighthouse—Life Long Love Affair" in The Keeper's Log, *winter 1987.*

Point Fermin Light Station in 1893. Courtesy of the U.S. Coast Guard.

Blackistone Island Light on the Potomac River, after it was disestablished (top) and as an active station (bottom). Top photo by A. Aubrey Bodine courtesy of The Mariners' Museum, Newport News, Virginia. Bottom photo courtesy of the U.S. Coast Guard. Burned in the 1950s, this station no longer exists.

XVIII. Josephine Freeman at Blackistone Island Light Station, Maryland, 1876-1912 ᠵ

Blackistone Island lies on the east side of the lower Potomac River. The 1850 owner, Dr. Joseph L. McWilliams, sold the southwest corner of the island to the U.S. government for $300 as a site for a lighthouse. Established in 1851, the Blackistone Island Light was kept from 1859 to 1868 by Dr. McWilliams's son Jerome. Dr. McWilliams himself kept the light from 1868 until 1875, when he turned it over to his daughter, Josephine.

In 1871 Josephine had married William 'Billie' Mitchell Freeman and lived on his farm on the Patuxent River until she moved back to Blackistone Island. Billie Freeman apparently gave up his farm to accompany her. Josephine's four surviving children were all born and grew up in the lighthouse—Bernard (1876); William, Jr. 'Willie' (1877); Emily (1880); and Edna (1882).

Josephine was paid $600 a year for keeping the light—the family's only steady income. She had no paid assistant and was responsible for both the light and the fog signal. She depended on her children to help her.

Josephine followed her father's example of writing a short record of each day's activities in an old-fashioned ledger. One surviving volume of her personal diary describes daily life in a rural lighthouse at the turn of the century. The diary began on November 16, 1903. *Today is Willie['s] Birthday, 26 years old. He is away from home on his vessel* Sarah Guyther*, he has been gone week today. I feel anxious about him, would like to hear from him . . .*

Josephine mentioned her own birthday as well on January 14, 1904. *I am 61 years old today. Thank God I have lived to be this old age. We had fruit cake & wine.*

Josephine recorded each visitor to the lighthouse, and there were many—neighbors, watermen, relatives, workmen, hunters, boaters sight-seeing—almost every day. In the summer there was daily visiting back and forth with the families who occupied the summer cottages on the island. Almost every entry described how they spent their evening—talking, playing cards, reading, writing, singing, listening to a gramaphone.

Josephine's children usually tended the lamp in the lighthouse lantern. January 12. *Will wicked the lamp up this morning.* January 18. *The lamp smoked this a.m. 3 o'clock. Willie had to get up & change the lamp. The tower was black with smoke. Willie & Ida* [the housekeeper] *washed it off. They were up there cleaning up until 12 o'clock. . . . Willie busy fixing the piece belongs in the top of the Tower & he painted it also.* January 26. *Willie wicked the big lamp & cleaned up the lamp* [lantern]*, etc.* May 13. *Willie wicked the Light House lamp this morning and he moved the stove out of the parlor.*

Willie did the work expected of a male keeper—making repairs and painting, as well as much of the maintenance around the lighthouse. April 6. *Willie cleaned the fog machinery today.* May 7. *Willie fixed winder* [window] *in the cellar. Put two panes in & one in his winder upstairs.* June 9. *Willie painting the tower this morning.* He painted the tower every spring.

After they moved into the lighthouse, Josephine's husband Billie occupied himself hunting and fishing, regularly providing their dinner. He hunted ducks every day throughout the fall and winter, weather permitting. Billie bred, trained, and sold hunting dogs. He kept a garden as well as cows, hogs, chickens, and turkeys. He did all the shopping, going regularly to the mainland to buy groceries, fruit, vegetables, and on rare occasions meat. He and his sons harvested and sold oysters, clams, and crabs. They did line fishing and put out gill and trap nets. They assisted neighbors in hauling nets, butchering livestock, and the like.

Josephine Freeman, keeper of Blackistone Island Light from 1876 until 1912. Courtesy of the St. Clement's Island - Potomac River Museum.

November 27. *Billie & Willie went up in the blind. Killed 12 ducks. . . . I am patching Billie's coat & Bernard's pants. All setting around the table talking. . . . Snow this evening, very bitter.*

Josephine, her daughters, and Ida made their own clothes, curtains, sheets and pillow cases, as well as the men's shirts and nightclothes. They also knitted, quilted, darned socks, and repaired all of their clothes. Josephine mended the sails for their various boats.

The rural area around Blackistone Island provided very little regular employment for young men. Josephine's sons and the two boys courting her daughters found a day's work now and then helping neighbors. June 17, 1904. *Willie gone up to the house to do day's work for Mr. Stephens, cutting grass & cleaning up. Very tired. Payed Willie $1 for his day's work.*

In September 1904 Bernard and Willie spent several days digging out a fresh-water pond on the island. It would be used when frozen to fill an ice house for the owner of the island. Billie and his sons sold the extra oysters and fish they harvested. But they seldom found any salaried employment.

December 1, 1903. . . . *Billie got up early to kill his hogs.* . . . For the next two days the whole family was busy cutting up meat, putting it in brine, cutting and drying the lard, making and smoking sausage.

December 26, 1903. . . . *Gale NW freezing. Willie had to get up 1:30 this morning to ring the bell. Rung until four a.m. . . .*

Fog was not unusual on the Potomac. The bell was rung by machinery, every 16 seconds, but it had to be wound up at regular intervals. January 13. *Willie singing & reading & ringing the bell until 2:30 p.m.* January 22. *Terrible day, fog & rain. Ringing bell most all day.*

On January 9 Josephine recorded one of the more dramatic events of the winter. A bell buoy broke away up the river and floated past the lighthouse. The boys tried to reach it and got thoroughly soaked breaking through the ice. They watched the buoy float up and down with the tide for the better part of a week until a tender finally came and took it back upriver.

Someone went over to the mainland to collect mail every day, weather permitting. Letters were so important that Josephine mentioned each letter they wrote and each one they received.

April 19. . . . *Billie & Willie went over to Coltons.* . . . *Wind blowing gale all day & still blowing gale. Billie will have to stay all night* . . .

The men, as well as Josephine's daughters, frequently stayed overnight when they went over to the mainland, particularly when the weather turned foul. With no means of communicating, Josephine had to assume they were all right. Visitors to the lighthouse often stayed the night as well. The girls' beaux stayed a week or two at a time, and nieces and nephews were there in the summer for weeks on end. An occasional boarder was accommodated. In September 1905 Josephine noted that they *had a houseful*—14 people staying overnight.

A tender stopped frequently at Blackistone Island. In October 1904 *the Lighthouse Tender* Holly *land[ed] 2 cord[s] of Oak wood.* July 29, 1905. *The Lighthouse Tender* Jessamine

*stop[p]ed at Station to see what repairs was needed &
measured how far the house was from the water & [left] plank
for the pumphouse, etc.* August 4. *Light House Tender*
Jessamine *stop[p]ed [at] station. Engineer brought carpenter
ashore & the lampist. Took measures, fence, etc. I got after
engineer to build me kitchen. They left dog here for Billie to
break.* August 25. *Lighthouse Tender* Holly *furnished 3 tons
coal & we had it put in the cellar.* August 28. *The tug* Thistle
*stop[p]ed [at the] Station with large lumber to build summer
kitchen . . . They took our pump out [of] the well to fix it.*
September 11. *The tug* Thistle, *Capt Smith, brought two
workmen over to the Lighthouse to finish the porch.*

On July 26, 1904, Josephine mentions lighting the lamp
herself for the first time. The children had all gone to
Leonardtown to the races and a dance in the evening—a major
outing. On the 29th, they all went to a dance at River Springs.
Dances were held every week in the summer in several
different places.

The women canned throughout the harvest season.
Josephine mentions making wine, seeding cherries and
canning them, pickling pears, making blackberry and grape
jam, crabapple jelly, tomato pickle, chillie sauce, and chow-
chow.

On November 7, election day, Billie, Willie, and Bernard
went to Coltons Point to meet Willie Herbert, *who would take
them up to the poles* [polls] *to vote in his spring wagon. . . .*

The last entry in the diary was made on November 9,
1905. *Willie Herbert* [who had recently married Edna] *is 21
years old today.*

Josephine Freeman continued as keeper of Blackistone
Island Light until her death in 1912 and was succeeded by her
son, William M. Freeman, Jr.

*This chapter is based on Josephine Freeman's 1903-05 diary, courtesy of
Barbara McWilliams.*

Kate McDougal, keeper of the Mare Island Light Station in California from 1881 to 1916, as a young woman. Courtesy of her granddaughter, Caroline Curtin.

The Mare Island Light Station around the turn of the century. The station no longer exists. Courtesy of Caroline Curtin.

XIX. Kate McDougal at Mare Island Light Station, California, 1881-1916 ᧒

Kate Coffee was born in 1842 in Florence, Alabama, daughter of a U.S. Army officer from an old Southern family. She grew up in New Orleans. Her father's assignments took the family eventually to San Francisco. There Kate showed her independence at an early age by marrying a northern naval officer, Charles J. McDougal, in the year following the end of the Civil War.

Some time in the 1870s Commander McDougal was appointed Inspector of the 12th Lighthouse District, which comprised the California coast. Among his duties was the inspection of lighthouses, the delivery of supplies from the lighthouse tender, and the paying of the keepers. In 1881 the lighthouse tender dinghy foundered as he and six others were landing through the heavy surf at the lighthouse at Cape Mendocino. Commander McDougal tried to swim to shore, but currents carried him away and the heavy money belt he wore around his waist dragged him under the waves. Kate was widowed, with four children between the ages of 8 and 14 and a pension of $50 a month.

Although the Navy provided little for widows, it did try to take care of its own. Charles McDougal's father had been commandant of the Mare Island Naval Shipyard, and relatives were still living there. Charles's Naval Academy classmate George Dewey (of later Spanish-American War fame) arranged for Kate's appointment as keeper of a new lighthouse. It was constructed in 1873 near the point where the Napa River enters Carquinez Strait and flows into San Pablo Bay.

The lighthouse was perched on a high cliff, with a long flight of stairs down to the pier. Lighthouse tenders came to this pier every three or four months to leave supplies—oil for the light, food, and in the early days, fresh water. Supplies were winched up the cliff in a wheeled cart on rails. At the end of the pier was the fogbell, which the keeper activated whenever fog crept across the bay. The light could never be left unattended. It had to be lit every night of the year, and a constant watch kept day and night for approaching fog.

Because of their isolation on Mare Island, family members provided their own social life. Relatives from the Bay area came occasionally to make extended visits. Trips were made by horse and buggy to the Naval Shipyard.

There was no school on the island, nor was it possible to travel daily from the lighthouse to the mainland. Kate McDougal educated her own children. Her teaching, with some extra tutoring in math, was good enough to prepare her son for the Naval Academy.

Kate's granddaughter remembered the base of the lantern tower being lined with shelves of books, many of them gifts from friends and relatives. All the Oz books were there, the Little Colonel series, and many sets of classics.

Kate and her eldest daughter loved flowers and planted a beautiful rose garden in front of the lighthouse. They probably also grew their own vegetables. Kate employed a laborer to do the heavy maintenance work, move the oil cart, and care for the cows. Someone built a two-room playhouse in the yard for the children, complete with glass windows, wooden floor, and even some cast-off furniture.

The officers at the Naval Shipyard who had known her husband kept track of Kate and assisted her when they could. During her first year on duty, these men put up poles and ran a telephone line from the shipyard to the lighthouse as a Christmas gift for her.

Kate was not a particularly enthusiastic housekeeper, much preferring her duties as light keeper. A Chinese-American cook prepared most of the meals. Occasionally the wife of one of the ranks at the shipyard came to do

Kate McDougal after her retirement as keeper of Mare Island Light Station in 1916. Courtesy of her granddaughter, Caroline Curtin.

housework. Every night Kate opened the curtains in the lantern and lit the light. The last person who went to bed was responsible for placing a fresh lamp inside the lens.

Kate spent a great deal of time making and recycling clothes for the children. Only the eldest daughter had new dresses. When she outgrew them, they were carefully taken apart, all pieces of material brushed clean and reversed, then reassembled for the next sister. Sometimes, if the material was still not too worn after use by three sisters, pants or jackets were made for brother Douglas.

Because no doctors or dentists were within easy reach, Kate patched and nursed her children as best she could. When her son decided to experiment with the effect of fire on dynamite, a piece of his ear was blown off. Kate sewed it back on with a needle and black thread.

Kate's eldest daughter married a naval officer. While he was away during the Spanish-American War, his wife and daughter returned to Mare Island to live in the lighthouse. The son-in-law stayed with them between assignments.

After her two older sisters married, Kate's third daughter assumed many of the domestic duties in the household. Young Caroline learned at an early age to clean, do laundry, cook on the wood stove, care for and milk the cow, churn butter, groom the horse, and drive the buggy to the ferry to make trips to town for necessities.

In 1910 a new light (Carquinez Strait Lighthouse) was established across the mouth of the Napa River, eliminating the need for the Mare Island Light. It was abandoned in 1917 and razed some time after 1930.

Kate retired in 1916 when an automatic fog signal was installed. She went to live with Caroline, who was married to the medical officer stationed at the Mare Island Naval Shipyard. Kate died in 1931.

⋯⊷⊜⊶⋯

Information in this chapter was gathered from Kate's granddaughter, Caroline Curtin; Annual Reports of the Light-House Board; *and Ralph Shanks,* Guardians of the Golden Gate *(Petaluma, California: Costano Books, 1990).*

XX. Laura Hecox at Santa Cruz Light Station, California, 1883-1917 ∽

Laura Hecox was born in 1854 in Santa Cruz. At an early age she tagged along after her father, exploring the tidal pools and sandy beaches along the northern edge of Monterey Bay. She gathered shells, rocks, minerals, and fossils. She was delighted when her father became keeper of the new Santa Cruz Lighthouse in 1869, for then she lived on the very shore of her beloved bay. Adna Hecox taught his younger children (Laura was the ninth) to help him tend the light.

Had Laura been born a hundred years later, she probably would have gone to college and become a marine biologist. Instead, by the time she reached her twenties, Laura was an amateur student of conchology. She corresponded with other shell collectors and exchanged specimens. She also increasingly assumed the duties of caring for the light as her father aged and his health failed.

In 1883 Adna Hecox died. Laura was 29. Her brother- in-law, Captain Albert Brown, recommended to federal officials in San Francisco that Laura be appointed keeper because she knew the duties. Within a week the appointment was made with a salary of $750 a year.

Laura lived in the lighthouse for a total of 47 years. Three of her siblings were married there, and three members of the Hecox family died there. In later years one of Laura's brothers came back to live in the lighthouse, as did a sister and her husband. Laura took care of her mother until she died in 1908 at age 92.

The light station was an ideal post for a conscientious young woman who loved collecting natural artifacts. In an 1896

Laura Hecox kept the Santa Cruz Light Station at the north end of Monterey Bay in California from 1883 to 1917. This station no longer exists. Courtesy of the National Archives, #26-LG-67-40.

booklet entitled *Beautiful Santa Cruz County*, Phil Francis writes that "The lighthouse is open to the inspection of the public three days in the week, and Miss Hecox not only exhibits to visitors the curious and costly mechanism of the great lamp, but takes pleasure in showing her own fine and interesting collection of marine curiosities. . . ."

The lamps in the Santa Cruz lantern were fueled before 1870 by high-quality lard oil. The oil was filtered from a half-gallon reservoir located up near the wick so that the heat would keep the oil fluid in cool weather. Lard oil was becoming very expensive—57 cents a gallon, compared to 8 ½ cents per gallon for kerosene. Santa Cruz Light was one of the first to be converted to the new fuel. An oil house to hold the very flammable liquid was not constructed until 1907. The wooden shelves in the tiny concrete structure (5 feet by 8 feet) held 120 five-gallon cans—a year's supply.

The light was focused to a plane 67 feet above sea level by a fourth-order Fresnel lens, about one and one-half feet in diameter, with 18 levels of polished flint glass prisms. Laura kept the lamps, the lens, and the lighthouse in pristine condition. A writer visiting in 1904 described Laura as "a most pleasant little woman, standing guard at the front door, armed

Laura Hecox, keeper of the Santa Cruz Light, enjoyed collecting rock specimens. Courtesy of the Santa Cruz Museum of Natural History.

with a big feather duster." A dusty-looking visitor got a brisk whisking before being admitted inside. Laura Hecox took the *Instructions to Light-Keepers* very seriously:

> The utmost neatness of buildings and premises is demanded. Bedrooms, as well as other parts of the dwelling, must be neatly kept. Untidiness will be strongly reprehended, and its continuance will subject a keeper to dismissal. The premises must be kept clean and well whitewashed; grounds in order; all the inside painted work of the lanterns well washed, and, when required, retouched with paint.

One entire room in the six-room house became Laura's private museum. There she arranged historical artifacts as well as biological specimens. She filled scrapbooks with clippings on taxidermy, architecture, literature, archeology, stamp collecting, astronomy, religion, geology, botany, and California history.

When a new public library was constructed in Santa Cruz in 1902, Laura Hecox was persuaded to donate her entire collection for permanent display. The Hecox Museum opened in 1905, and included exhibit cases devoted to dried starfish, crustaceans, Indian baskets and mortars, Eskimo artifacts, minerals, agates, gems, South Sea island curios, petrified woods, coral, shells, and turtle and tortoise carapaces.

After her mother's death, Laura remained in the small white keeper's house, faithfully tending the light, until her retirement in 1917 at age 63. Her death followed two years later.

Source material was collected from the Santa Cruz City Museum of Natural History; Frank Perry, Lighthouse Point: Reflections on Monterey Bay History *(Soquel, California: GBH Publishing 1982); and* 1902 Instructions to Light-Keepers.

XXI. Kate Walker at Robbins Reef Light Station, New York, 1890-1919 ॐ

On the west side of the main channel into the inner harbor of New York City, a mile from Staten Island, is a hidden ridge of rocks that once caused numerous shipwrecks and great loss of life. In 1839 a lighthouse was built on Robbins Reef to guide large ships to New York City wharves.

In 1883 the Light-House Board replaced the old stone tower with a four-tier cone-shaped iron structure. The light in the 56-foot tower was magnified by a fourth-order Fresnel lens. A flashing mechanism revolved between the stationary lantern and the outside windows, rotated by a slowly descending weight that made the light flash brightly every six seconds. The light could be seen for 12 miles, except on foggy nights. It was one of the first lights the pilot of an incoming vessel saw when he entered Ambrose Channel. It showed him the way up through the Kill van Kull to Newark Bay, or on past the much brighter Statue of Liberty Light to the Port of New York.

The keeper's quarters fitted around the base of the tower like a donut. The kitchen and dining room were on the main floor. Lockers for clothes and closets for china fitted into the sides of the iron cone. Two bedrooms were on the smaller floor above.

The area of rock above water was hardly larger than the lighthouse itself and provided no mooring for boats. The keeper's skiff hung in davits from the platform. Access to the keeper's quarters was by a steel ladder rising out of the water up to the kitchen door.

To help mariners identify lighthouses in the 19th century, towers were painted in a distinctive combination of colors.

These were listed in a *Light List* made available to any navigator by the Lighthouse Service. The Robbins Reef tower was painted white above and brown below—as it still is today.

The second keeper of the light in the new iron tower was John Walker. He had been assistant keeper at Sandy Hook Light. There in the boarding house where he ate his meals, he met a German immigrant woman waiting table. He taught her English, married her, and took her to Sandy Hook. John Walker's bride was in many ways typical of the working women who by 1870 made up one-quarter of all wage earners in the United States. They were either young single women or widows with children to support—many of them immigrants or children of immigrants. Kate, an immigrant with a fatherless child, married a working-class man.

John Walker received the keeper's appointment on Robbins Reef in 1885 with a $600 annual salary. Kate's first look at the tiny foothold in the channel made her threaten to leave him. "When I first came to Robbins Reef, the sight of water, which ever way I looked, made me lonesome. I refused to unpack my trunks at first, but gradually, a little at a time, I unpacked. After a while they were all unpacked and I stayed on."

In 1890 John Walker, ill with pneumonia, was rowed to the mainland in the lighthouse dinghy by Kate's young son. His last words to his wife were, "Mind the light, Katie." So she stayed and tended the light. When he died ten days later, a substitute was sent so that Kate could attend his funeral, but she was back on the job before the day ended.

Several men were offered Walker's post but turned it down because Robbins Reef was too lonely. When Kate, then 42 years old with two children to care for, applied for the keeper's appointment, objections were raised because she was only four feet, ten inches tall and weighed barely 100 pounds. Kate was paid as a laborer until 1894. She finally received the official keeper's appointment in June 1894. Her son Jacob was appointed assistant keeper in 1896.

Time proved that Kate was as good at her job as any man. She not only kept the light burning, but rescued as many

Robbins Reef Light Station on the west side of New York Upper Bay, marking shoal water on the New Jersey side of the main channel to the Manhattan docks. Courtesy of the U.S. Coast Guard.

as 50 people by her own count—mostly fishermen whose boats were blown onto the reef by sudden storms. One such incident was the wreck of a three-masted schooner that struck the reef and rolled over onto its side. Kate launched her dinghy and took aboard the five crew members, plus a small Scottie dog, whose survival pleased her enormously.

Among other flotsam brought to Robbins Reef by the tide, Kate Walker hauled in a small box containing the dead body of a half-dressed baby, with its little hands stretched out as though appealing for help. She lowered the rowboat from the davits and took the lifeless body over to the coroner on Staten Island. Its identity was never determined.

When the light was obscured by fog, as it frequently was in winter, Kate went down into the deep basement and started the engine that sent out siren blasts from a foghorn at intervals of three seconds. The siren made so much noise that she and her son didn't even try to sleep. Occasionally the foghorn machinery broke down. Then Kate climbed to the top of the tower and banged a huge bell. When the men at the lighthouse station on Staten Island heard the bell, they knew they must visit Robbins Reef and make repairs as soon as wind and weather permitted.

In winter Kate removed frost from inside the glass windows, and during snowstorms climbed outside onto the balcony to clear away the snow. The official instructions were: "To prevent the frosting of the plate glass of lanterns, put a small quantity of glycerin on a linen cloth and rub it over the inner surface of the glass. One application when the lamp is lighted and another at midnight will generally be found sufficient to keep the glass clear during the night."

In her years at Robbins Reef Kate Walker saw the progression from kerosene lamps to incandescent oil vapor lamps (similar to today's Coleman lantern) to electricity. The Light-House Board began experimenting with electric lights in the 1880s, and gradually converted those lighthouses located near power lines.

A *New York Times* reporter described Kate Walker's life in 1906:

> Mrs. Walker . . . spends as much time on the terrace outside of her house as she does indoors, even when the wind blows and the salt spray compels her to don an oilskin jacket and a sou'wester. . . .
>
> Mrs. Walker serves tea [on the balcony] when the bay is smooth enough for her friends to go out in rowboats to see her. In the Winter, when the water is rough and the

Kate Walker, who lived at the Robbins Reef Light Station off Staten Island in New York Harbor from 1885 to 1919. Photo as it appeared in Harper's Weekly, *Volume 53, August 14, 1909. Courtesy of the Virginia State Library and Archives.*

lighthouse is surrounded with floating ice half the time, Mrs. Walker is virtually a hermit . . . .

Kate had a sewing machine and a wind-up phonograph. Her children played records, happy to hear the sound of a human voice.

Once a year a lighthouse tender brought Kate six tons of coal, a few barrels of oil, and a pay envelope. Other than an occasional inspector's visit, she received little official attention unless the fog signal broke down. The *Times* article emphasized the limits of her horizons:

> All that she knows from personal experience of the great land to which she came as a girl immigrant from Germany is , . . . Staten Island, New York City, and Brooklyn. She says she has never wanted to go West, South, or anywhere else. . . . As a wife, mother, and widow, the happiest and saddest days of her peaceful life have been spent within the circular walls of her voluntary prison. . . .

Kate Walker resented any implication that, because she was a lighthouse keeper, she had no household duties in common with other women.

> This lamp in the tower, it is more difficult to care for than a family of children. It need not be wound more than once in five hours, but I wind it every three hours so as to take no chances. In nineteen years that light has never disappointed sailors who have depended upon it. Every night I watch it until 12 o'clock. Then, if all is well, I go to bed, leaving my assistant [her son Jacob] in charge.

Jacob had come from Germany with his mother. He was his mother's postman, marketman, and general courier. Kate and John Walker's daughter Mamie boarded with a family on the mainland when it was time to go to school. Jacob also spent much of his time ashore after his marriage.

The lighthouse historian Edward Rowe Snow, in his book entitled *Famous Lighthouses of America*, tells another story about Kate Walker—of a Christmas evening that turned into one of her most frightening experiences when a gale blew in:

> I knew that to the people coming through the Narrows the snow would hide the light. When I started the foghorn, the snow changed to sleet and drove against the windows. Then, above the driving of the sleet and the rattling of the wind, I heard a sound that I had heard but twice in twenty-five years and dreaded hearing.
>
> We kept our rowboat fastened to the outside walls by a chain, and if that chain broke, and the noise indicated that perhaps it had, I would be helpless to leave the tower.

I wrapped myself up well and went outside. The wind nearly whirled me off the landing, while the sleet covered my hair like a hood. I felt my way along the icy walls. As I thought, one of the chains had been forced loose, and just then the loose end hit me in the eye. But I secured the boat and fought my way back toward the door.

The gale blew in my face as I passed the iron ladder, and began to force me off the balcony. I knew that I could never get a foothold on the icy rungs of the ladder should the wind push me from the balcony. Finally I had to sink to my knees, and work my way to the door where I pushed it open, crawled inside, and shut and locked it. I knew my children would not attempt to return that evening, and so I spent Christmas that night alone in the lighthouse.

Assisted by her son, Kate tended the Robbins Reef Light until her retirement in 1919 at age 73. Then she lived in a small frame cottage in Tompkinsville on Staten Island. She died in 1931. Her obituary in the *New York Evening Post* contained a moving passage:

A great city's water front is rich in romance. . . . There are the queenly liners, the grim battle craft, the countless carriers of commerce that pass in endless procession. And amid all this and in sight of the city of towers and the torch of liberty lived this sturdy little woman, proud of her work and content in it, keeping her lamp alight and her windows clean, so that New York Harbor might be safe for ships that pass in the night.

Today, the Robbins Reef light is automated, and the lighthouse is closed to the public. In 1996 the Coast Guard launched a buoy tender named in Kate's honor.

⊷⟹⟸⊷

Sources for this chapter include The New York Times, *March 4 and 5, 1906;* The Staten Island Historian, *1978;* American Magazine, *October 1925;* Clifford Gallant, "Mind the Light, Katie" in The Keeper's Log, *summer 1987;* Carol Bird, "The Loneliest Woman in the World," Philadelphia Ledger, *August 23, 1925; U.S. Department of Transportation* News, CG 21-96.

Port Pontchartrain Light Station on Lake Pontchartrain in Louisiana, kept by Ellen Wilson and Margaret Norvell. Courtesy of the National Archives, #26-LG-37-51.

XXII. Ellen Wilson at Port Pontchartrain Light Station, Louisiana, 1882-1896; Margaret Norvell at Head of Passes Light Station, 1891-1896, at Port Pontchartrain Light Station, 1896-1924, and at New Canal Light Station, Louisiana, 1924-1932 ♌

A memo dated April 10, 1882, to the Chairman of the Light-House Board from the Light-House Inspector in New Orleans gave rather unusual reasons for nominating a woman keeper:

> Regarding the vacancy at Port Pontchartrain caused by the resignation of David F. Power, Keeper: I have requested the Collector of Customs, New Orleans, to nominate Mrs. Ellen Wilson to fill the vacancy, and he has kindly consented to do so.
>
> In explanation, I wish to say that Mrs. Wilson is a widow, with no resources except her own labor, and the mother of Mrs. Young, wife of the clerk in this office.
>
> Mr. Young, as is well known to the Board, has done efficient and faithful service here for over fifteen years, and I have requested the nomination of Mrs. Wilson in his interest.
>
> The circumstances are such that he can seldom get away from New Orleans, and this appointment, besides giving a support to a worthy woman who will perform the duty well, will afford him and his family a convenient place for recreation and a place of refuge in case of epidemic. His services, I think, entitle him to some recognition, and I particularly desire that the appointment be made.

Ellen Wilson kept the Port Pontchartrain light from 1882 until 1896.

⚬⟹⟸⚬

Margaret Norvell carried on her husband Louis's duties as official keeper of Head of Passes Light in Louisiana after he drowned in 1891. This was a surprising career for a woman who came from a well-known New Orleans family and married a well-to-do cotton dealer. The loss of his fortune led the Norvells into the Lighthouse Service.

In 1896 Margaret was appointed official keeper of the Port Pontchartrain Light Station on Lake Pontchartrain in Louisiana, following Ellen Wilson.

The lighthouse was located near the east terminus of the Pontchartrain Railroad, where the town of Milneburg was a transfer point for goods and a stop-over for passengers on the way to and from the lake's north shore health resorts. The tower elevated the light 35 feet above sea level, making it visible 10 miles. According to a *Times Picayune* article in 1934, Margaret kept chickens and a Spitz dog in her yard, and a talking parrot in her kitchen. Her living room was lined with books and graced by a piano. She brought up her two children in the lighthouse.

An account of Madge Norvell's career in the *Morning Tribune* of June 26, 1932, recounts the many lives she saved. "I have often rung my fogbell," she said, "to get help for overturned boats or to signal directions to yachts." During one storm, she threw a rope to the crews of both a yacht and a schooner, bringing them safely into the lighthouse and providing food and shelter for several days until the storm abated. On other occasions she rescued people from disabled sailboats and from a small plane blown into the lake in a squall. The article goes on:

> It is not only the shipwrecked to whom Mrs. Norvell opened her doors. In every big hurricane or storm here since 1891, her lighthouse has been a refuge for fishermen and others whose homes have been swept away. In the . . . storm of 1903 Mrs. Norvell's lighthouse was the only building left standing on the lower coast, and over 200

survivors found a welcome and shelter in her home. After each storm she started the relief funds and helped the poor folk get back to normal.

Madge must have learned to love the lights. After her retirement she went every evening at sunset to the seawall to watch for the first flashing of the beacon she had tended. In her own words, "there isn't anything unusual in a woman keeping a light in her window to guide men folks home. I just happen to keep a bigger light than most women because I have got to see that so many men get safely home."

The light at Port Pontchartrain was discontinued in 1929 and the tower turned over to the Orleans Parish Levee Board. Newspaper accounts of Margaret's death in 1934 indicated that she also tended the electrified light in the New Canal (West End) Light Station on Lake Pontchartrain from 1924 until 1932.

Material for this chapter was gathered from the National Archives Record Group 16, Entries 24 and 82; and clippings from files of the U.S. Lighthouse Society.

The Tabberrah family at Cumberland Head Light around 1880. This light was kept by Emma Tabberrah from 1904 until 1919. The station is now a private residence. Photo made from a tintype belonging to Arthur B. Hillegas.

XXIII. Emma Tabberrah at Cumberland Head Light Station, New York, 1904-1919 ༈

Because William Tabberrah was a disabled veteran of the Civil War, he was given the position of keeper of the light at Cumberland Head on Lake Champlain in 1871. His wife Emma brought two babies to the new limestone-block quarters beside the much older conical tower. Six more Tabberrah children were born in the lighthouse.

In spite of his disability, William kept the light for 33 years. He purchased an 89-acre farm adjoining the lighthouse property, which enabled him to indulge his love of horses. The nearest town, Plattsburgh, was seven miles away, requiring horse-and-buggy transportation to reach it.

William was continually plagued by a lead bullet lodged in his hip. In 1903, surgery to remove the bullet led to an infection that killed him. Emma applied for his job and was appointed keeper in 1904 at a salary of $480 a year. She served until her retirement in 1919 (when she received a pension of $190.17 per year). Two of her daughters kept her company and assisted her with her keeper's duties.

The towerwas 50 feet high, putting the focal beam from the Fresnel lens 75 feet above the lake level and making it visible for 11 miles. An oil room connected the tower to the keeper's house and served to store kerosene and lamps as well as a workbench and tools. The daily cleaning and maintenance of the lamps was done there.

The first floor of the keeper's house had a parlor, a dining-sitting room, and a pantry. The kitchen was in a one-story addition at the back of the house. Upstairs were two large and two small bedrooms, above them an unfinished attic. Wood stoves in the kitchen and the sitting room heated the house. An outbuilding contained a carriage house, a stable for two horses, a woodshed, and an outhouse. In the 19th century the family did without plumbing, electricity, or a telephone.

Had Emma Tabberrah recorded her memories, she doubtless would have outlined her lighthouse duties. But what her children remembered and passed on to their children were the charming details of family life in a rural lighthouse at the turn of the century. Rain water for household washing and bathing was collected in a basement cistern and pumped by hand into the kitchen sink. The well water on the property had a heavy concentration of sulphur, giving it a strong taste. Emma was the only one who liked it well enough to drink it. The others brought drinking water in pails from Lake Champlain.

Fortunately the local school was only a mile away so the children could walk, ski, or snowshoe up through the woods behind their home to the main road. As they grew older, three of the girls boarded in Plattsburgh while taking teacher training. As for playmates, there were very few neighbors except for summer residents in the cottages on Lake Champlain. The children were always overjoyed when cousins came to spend summer holidays at the lighthouse.

The family provided its own entertainment. The children learned to identify the woodland animals and birds. They often cared for injured birds. They played croquet on the lawn and tennis on their homemade court. They cultivated the garden and went on outings to gather flowers and berries. In the summer they could fish and sail on the lake and take picnics to the beach, and in winter they went ice-boating. The girls learned sewing and embroidery as well as cooking. The boys helped their father operate the farm.

The family had a piano and their father played the flute. On Sunday afternoons Emma dressed in her best gown and received callers in the parlor. Guests were offered refreshments. The children loved nothing better than bringing ice (cut from the lake in the winter and stored in an ice house in the woods) to pack into a hand-cranked ice cream freezer. They took turns turning the crank and licking the paddles when it was done.

Emma Tabberrah, keeper of the Cumberland Head Light Station, after her retirement. Courtesy of her grandson, Arthur B. Hillegas.

In 1904 the Tabberrahs' daughter Rose married Milo Hillegas under the walnut tree on the lighthouse lawn. This happy occasion was followed only three months later by her father's death. He had been bedridden for two years, requiring Emma to be both constant nurse and keeper of the light.

After her 15 years keeping the Cumberland Head Light, Emma retired and spent another 14 years with her daughter Maud in Beekmantown, devoting her days to her children and grandchildren. She was buried beside her husband in Plattsburgh, New York.

In 1934 a skeleton tower was built by the lake shore to hold an automated acetylene light. The old lighthouse was no longer needed and was sold to private owners.

This chapter is primarily based on reminiscences of Arthur Burdette Hillegas, grandson of Emma Tabberrah.

Fannie Salter and her son feed turkeys on the lawn of Turkey Point Light Station (above) at the head of the Chesapeake Bay. Only the tower remains. Fannie Salter's daughter Mabel rings the fog bell in the 1930s (below). Courtesy of the Ralph Smith Collection, The Mariners' Museum, Newport News, Virginia.

XXIV. Fannie Salter at Turkey Point Light Station, Maryland, 1925-1947 ৯৲

The lighthouse at Turkey Point, Maryland, was built of dressed stone in 1833. Only 38 feet tall, its location on a bluff at the southern tip of Elk Neck is 100 feet above the bay, making the light visible for 13 miles.

Turkey Point Light Station was kept by women longer than any other light on the Chesapeake Bay. Elizabeth Lusby kept the light from 1844 to 1861, when she died at age 65. Rebecca Crouch was appointed keeper after her husband died in 1873, and served until 1895. She was succeeded by her daughter, Georgianna Crouch Brumfield, who remained until 1919.

Fannie Mae Salter was the last civilian woman to keep a light. When her keeper husband died in 1925, Fannie was told she was beyond the Civil Service age limit. She appealed to her senator, who went to the White House and asked President Coolidge to appoint her to the post. She was keeper at Turkey Point from 1925 until 1947.

Fannie Salter's logs are in the National Archives. Each day she recorded the weather, and, like Harriet Colfax, she occasionally added personal comments to her logs. Here are a few examples that show the routine of her daily life as she began her career as official keeper:

> April 1, 1925. *Northwest fresh, cloudy. Received telegram that I have been appointed as permanent keeper of this Station by Pres. Coolidge. Went to North East* [a nearby Maryland town] *for supplies. Painted in lantern. Cleaned lens to-day.*
>
> April 6. *Northeast fresh a.m., calm p.m. clear. Cleaned brass to-day.*

April 9. *Southwest moderate clear. Painted lantern floor & platform below. Unpacking furniture.*

April 16. *North to northeast fresh clear. Scrubbed lantern, cleaned cellar, pumped water out of boat.*

April 20. *Northeast fresh, cloudy clearing to west p.m. Keeper left 6:30 a.m. for Balto[imore] on official business. Returned same day 10:15 p.m.*

April 23. *Southwest rain in early morning, but cleared off pretty. Recharged fire extinguisher.*

April 27. *South to west light fair. Put screens in windows, shellacked two floors.*

April 29. *Northeast fresh cloudy. Pumped water out of boat. Scrubbed lantern floor.*

September 2. *West to southwest light, partly cloudy. Cleaned storm panes inside and out.*

September 5. *Northwest light, fair. Cleaned tower from top to bottom & bell house.*

September 8. *Light northwest partly cloudy. Mowed lawn.*

September 9. *Moderate southwest hazy. Tender Juniper delivered medicine, wheelbarrow & parts for stove.*

September 17. *West moderate, clear cool. Finished painting exterior of bell house.*

September 18. *Moderately southerly winds partly cloudy. Whitewashed interior of toilet, painted the wood.*

September 19. *West moderate fair. Painted tower floor, handrail and ladder, scrubbed tower steps.*

September 21. *Tender Maple arrived with wood & coal, also fogbell machinery, and Mr. Lenord came to install same.*

September 29. *Northwest light, partly cloudy. Painted new woodwork in bell house.*

The Lighthouse Service became part of the Coast Guard in 1939. Keepers were given the choice of joining the military or retiring when their current assignment ended.

Until 1943, when electricity was installed at Turkey Point, Fannie found it necessary to make four or five trips daily to the top of the tower. When a 100-watt electric bulb was placed inside the Fresnel lens, increasing the light to 680 candlepower, the keeper's time-consuming duties were reduced to the mere flip of a switch. Only in cold weather did the keeper make more

Fannie Salter and her Chesapeake Bay retriever go about chores at the Turkey Point Light Station. Courtesy of the Ralph Smith Collection, The Mariners' Museum, Newport News, Virginia.

than one trip to the tower to defrost the huge windows surrounding the light. The heavy brass oil lamps used earlier were kept ready in case the electric power and auxiliary plant should fail.

Like other lighthouse keepers, Fannie Salter maintained a radio watch and was on duty seven days a week, 24 hours a day. She was in constant communication with aids-to-navigation authorities. She made reports of local weather conditions and other necessary information by a radio telephone set, installed by the Coast Guard during World War II. Although no one showed her how to use it, Fannie mastered the radio with the aid of a manual.

Snow-blocked roads often stranded Fannie many weeks at a time during the winter, leaving radio and telephone as her only links with the outside world. She fed herself from her well-stocked vegetable cellar, where shelves were lined with home-canned jars of vegetables and fruits from her garden on the lighthouse's three-acre plot. A Chesapeake Bay retriever, a flock of chickens, and a dozen lambs and sheep were her company after her three children grew up. In the early years of Fannie's tenure, laundry, bakery, and ice trucks made deliveries to the lighthouse. World War II ended that.

"And when I get tired of things outdoors, I always have my hobby—crossword puzzles, " Fannie said. "My friends send me many hundreds, but I'm always 'fresh out'. Most of my evenings are spent on crossword puzzles and reading."

Bradley, Fannie's youngest child, helped her with some of the heavier chores around the light station.

Talking over her early days as keeper of the light at Turkey Point, Fannie recalled one of her most frightening experiences. "It was a cold night and very foggy out," she said. "I was alone with my seven-year-old son at the time. Suddenly

Fannie Salter polishes the Fresnel lens in the lantern of Turkey Point Light. Courtesy of the U.S. Coast Guard.

Fannie Salter holds an electric light bulb and the incandescent oil lamp which the bulb replaced. Courtesy of the U.S. Coast Guard.

the whistle of a boat, apparently making for Philadelphia, was heard around our point. I started the bell ringing, but almost immediately a cable connected to the striking mechanism snapped.

"I began to pull the bell, counting to fifteen between each pull. It was necessary to ring the bell four times a minute. I kept this up for about 55 minutes, until the ship was safely around the point and headed for the Chesapeake and Delaware Canal."

Modern floating aids to navigation did away with the need for a fogbell, but Fannie's duties included visually checking and reporting on the various buoys, channel lights, and other aids she could see from her tower so they were kept in proper position and working order.

When Fannie finally retired in 1947, she moved to a house six miles away, where she could still see her beloved light flashing. Later she lived in Baltimore where she died in 1966 at age 83.

Fannie Salter lowers the flag at Turkey Point Light. Courtesy of the U.S. Coast Guard.

At Turkey Point, the Coast Guard tore down the outbuildings and the keeper's house, also destroying the brick stairway in the tower so that vandals could not reach the light. The light was deactivated in 2000; a local friends group now maintains the station.

⊷⟞⟝⊶

Sources for this chapter include W. W. Wilson, Coast Guard press release issued in 1945; Olga Crouch of North East, Maryland, Fannie Salter's granddaughter; Robert O. Smith, "Fannie Salter—America's Last Woman Lighthouse Keeper" in The Weather Gauge *(date unknown);* The Sunday Star Pictorial Magazine, *April 20, 1947; and obituary in the* Mobile Press Register, *March 13, 1966.*

Epilogue ॐ

Automation of the lights meant that resident keepers were no longer needed, but the lighthouses themselves still delight us. In our imagination we can see storm-tossed seamen watching for the light that will guide them safely to a harbor.

Much work is required to maintain these reminders of a more hazardous past. The Coast Guard tries to find custodians who will preserve both automated and deactivated stations. Some stations have been turned into marine research laboratories or bed-and-breakfast inns. Historical societies and local authorities have promised to preserve, interpret, and keep intact the lighthouses in their communities. The lighthouse is turned into a museum or a historic site that permit hundreds of visitors to explore them.

Although in many cases only the grounds of the stations are open to the public, you can still climb some of the towers and see the old Fresnel lens displayed. There you can form a mental picture of the sturdy keeper going about his duties.

Probably you imagined hard-working men lighting and watching the lights night after night, regardless of monotony or heavy weather. But you know now that dozens of brave women also climbed those stairs and lit those lamps and polished those lenses. Their dedication to the safety of the ships that plied our coasts and waterways matched that of the male keepers. Remember them as well and honor them for their courage and devotion.

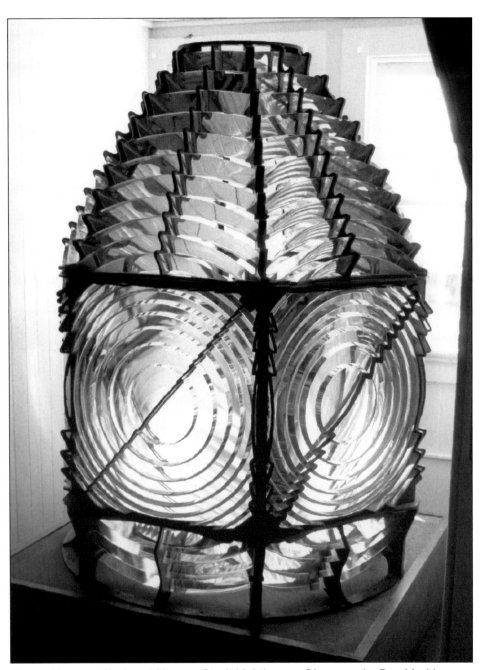

Fresnel lens on display at Hooper Strait Lighthouse, Chesapeake Bay Maritime Musesum. National Park Service photo by Candace Clifford.

Glossary ༀ

£6.13.4 – English money: 6 pounds, 13 shillings, and 4 pence.

acetylene-powered light – A lamp powered by acetylene, a colorless, highly flammable gas, C2H2.

aerobeacons with a 1,000-watt lamp – Powerful lights used at airports to direct planes. These were mounted on poles at many lighthouses, replacing the light in the lantern.

aid to navigation – Any stationary marker placed to guide ships: lighthouse, beacon, lightship, buoy, channel marker, etc.

Ambrose Channel – The main channel for ships leaving the Atlantic to enter the Port of New York.

Annual Report of the Light-House Board – An annual report issued by the United States Light-House Board after 1852, summarizing its activities.

Argand lamp – Invented by an Englishman, a fountain lamp consisting of an oil reservoir, a burner with a hollow circular wick and lamp chimney, and a parabolic reflector.

assistant keeper – A person appointed to assist a head keeper in the duties of maintaining a light station. Some stations had two or three assistants.

automated beacon – A light that is turned on and off by a light sensor, without the need for a human presence.

balustrade – A rail and the row of posts that support it.

barometer – An instrument for measuring atmospheric pressure.

bowsprit – A spar extending forward from the stem of a sailing ship.

buoy – A float moored or a spindle driven in water as a warning of danger under the surface or as a marker for a channel.

buoy tender – A vessel that is used to place and maintain buoys and other aids to navigation; formerly referred to as a 'lighthouse tender'.

caisson – A watertight structure within which construction work is carried out. With lighthouses, the caisson forms the base on which the tower is erected.

chandelier – In lighthouses, a circular fixture suspended from the ceiling that holds a number of light bulbs or lamps.

channel lights – Lights, usually on buoys, that mark a navigable ship channel.

characteristic of a light – Each light can be distinguished from all others by its characteristic. It may be fixed (unchanging) or revolving; flashing at set intervals, which differ from light to light; colored white or red, etc. Each light's characteristics are published in a *Light List* available to all mariners. When a light's characteristics are changed, a *Notice to Mariners* is published in local newspapers.

cistern – A receptacle or tank for collecting and holding water or other liquid.

Civil Service – All branches of public service that are not legislative, judicial, military, or naval. Collectively, the persons employed by these branches.

collector of customs – The person employed to collect the duties or taxes imposed on imported and, less commonly, exported goods. Some collectors also served as superintendent of lighthouses.

colonial militia – In the American colonies under British rule, a citizen army, as distinct from a body of professional soldiers.

davits – Any of various types of small cranes used to hoist boats, anchors, and cargo.

daymark – A unique pattern or shape that distinguishes one lighthouse from another.

dressed stone – Stone that has been shaped with tools so it can be tightly fitted together.

duck decoys – Life-size reproductions of ducks carved from wood, and floated by hunters to attract wild ducks.

elevation – With lighthouses, the distance above the ground to the light. (See **focal plane**)

first-order – Fresnel lenses came in several sizes, the largest (first-order) giving off the powerful light needed on headlands or an open seacoast. The smaller lenses (fourth-order, fifth-order, etc.) were suitable for marking harbors, bays, or obstructions—places where the light did not need to be seen at great distances.

fixed light – In a lighthouse, a light that is continuous and unchanging.

flashing mechanism – A clockwork or other means whereby a light is made to flash at set intervals.

flashing light – An aid to navigation that flashes at set intervals, such as every three seconds, five seconds, eight seconds, etc.

flat-wick lamp – Lamp lit by burning a flat strand of braided fibers that draws up fuel to the flame. Some lamps have round wicks.

focal plane – The height of the light in a lighthouse above sea level. This includes both the height of the tower and height of the land on which it sits.

focal point – A point on the axis of symmetry of an optical system, such as a Fresnel lens, to which parallel rays of light converge.

fog bell – A bell, whistle, horn, or siren used to warn ships of navigation hazards during foggy weather.

fog siren – A device in which compressed air or steam is driven against a rotating perforated disk to create a loud, penetrating whistle.

Fresnel lens – Invented in 1822 by a Frenchman named Fresnel, the glass lens surrounded the lamp in a lighthouse, with prisms at the top and bottom to refract the light into a powerful horizontal beam. The central prisms and drum (in the case of a fixed optic) or bull's eye (in the case of a rotating optic) also refracted the light into a horizontal beam, intensified by a powerful magnifying glass around the middle of the lens. Fresnel lenses came in several sizes: a first-order lens was the largest and gave off the powerful light needed on headlands or an open seacoast. The smaller lenses were suitable for marking harbors, bays, or obstructions—places where the light did not need to be seen at great distances.

frigate – A high-speed, medium-sized sailing war vessel of the 17th, 18th, and 19th centuries.

garrison – A military post or the troops stationed at such a post.

gunwales – The upper edge of a ship's side.

illuminating apparatus – Whatever was used in a lighthouse to produce the light in the lantern.

incandescent oil vapor lamp – A lamp in which a filament is heated to incandescence by an appropriate fuel.

instructions to lightkeepers – Instructions issued by whoever was in charge of the Lighthouse Service, telling the keepers how to perform their duties.

keeper's dwelling/quarters – On a light station, the building or buildings in which the keeper or keepers lived.

kerosene/mineral oil – A thin oil distilled from petroleum or shale oil, used as a fuel.

lampist – In the Lighthouse Service, an individual specially trained to service and repair the optics or lighting mechanisms.

landmark – Any prominent and identifying feature of a landscape that can serve as a daymark.

lantern – In a lighthouse, the glass-paned cage at the top of the tower within which the light is protected from the weather.

lanthorn – An earlier spelling of "lantern."

lard oil – An oil that comes from the white solid or semisolid fat of a hog.

"Lighthouse Keepers and Assistants" – A hand-written register of the appointments of light keepers and assistant keepers in the 19th century. Now located in the National Archives and available on microfilm.

lighthouse tender – A vessel used to carry supplies and personnel to lighthouses and to tend other aids to navigation, such as buoys and lightships.

Lighthouse Service – A generic term that has been used to include all the people involved in operating lighthouses.

lighthouse keeper – The resident individual appointed to maintain the light at a light station.

lighthouse engineer – Under the United States Light-House Board, an Army officer assigned to a Light-House District to oversee construction and maintenance of light stations within that district.

lighthouse inspector – Under the United States Light-House Board, a Navy officer assigned to a Light-House District to oversee hiring and daily administration at the field level.

lightship – In dangerous locations at sea where a lighthouse could not be built, a ship that was anchored permanently in one spot, displaying a light from masts on the deck.

mariner – A sailor.

mourning period – A length of time after a death in the family during which family members refrained from social activities.

National Archives – The federal agency in which government papers are housed after they are no longer being actively used. The main facility in is Washington, DC: <www.archives.gov>

oil house – The small building that was added to light stations after the adoption of kerosene as a fuel to keep the very flammable fuel away from other buildings.

oil butt – A large cask or canister in which oil was kept.

pilot – Someone licensed to guide ships in and out of ports. Not a member of the ship's crew.

prefabricated cast iron – Liquid iron formed into a particular shape by pouring it into a mold.

public works – Construction projects, such as highways or dams, paid for by public funds and constructed by the government for the benefit or use of the general public.

radio beacon – A fixed radio transmitter that broadcasts distinctive signals as a navigational aid.

radio telephone – A telephone in which audible communication is established by radio.

radio watch – Constant communication with the nearest Coast Guard Station by means of a radio telephone.

reflectors – In 19th-century lighthouses an oval metal pan, usually coated with silver and placed behind an Argand or Lewis lamp to increase the brightness of the light.

revenue cutter – A sailing vessel or steamer used in the 19th century to aid in collecting customs on shipping. In 1915 the U.S. Revenue Cutter Service merged with the U.S. Life-Saving Service to form the U.S. Coast Guard.

revolving light/rotating light – A mechanism which turned a lighthouse lens in circles, producing a flashing light.

rheumatism – A joint disease today known as arthritis.

rod – A linear measure equal to 5.5 yards, 16.03 feet, or 5.03 meters.

rubblestone – Irregular fragments or pieces of unshaped rock used in masonry construction.

schooner – A sailing ship with two or more masts, the mainmast being behind and taller than the foremast.

Secretary of the Treasury – The official in a president's cabinet who is in charge of the Treasury Department. The Lighthouse Service was under the Treasury Secretary from 1790 to 1901.

seeding oyster beds – Planting oyster sprat in the water where they will grow until they reach maturity and can be harvested.

skeleton or skeletal tower – A tower constructed of metal struts and cross braces to hold a lantern on its top.

skiff – A flat-bottomed open boat of shallow draft, having a pointed bow and a square stern.

sperm or whale oil – Combustible oil made from the fat of the sperm whale.

Stephen Pleasonton – The Fifth Auditor of the Treasury Department who was placed in charge of the Lighthouse Establishment from 1820 to 1852.

superintendent of lighthouses – A title given to collectors of customs after they were given the supervision of the lighthouses in their districts.

tide – The periodic variation in the surface level of the oceans caused by the gravitational attraction of the sun and moon.

trimming the wick – The burned part of a lamp wick had to be trimmed away periodically to ensure maximum brightness of the flame.

twin lights – Light stations that display two or more lights to distingush them from stations nearby.

United States Light-House Board – A board appointed in 1852 to take responsibility for upgrading and maintaining the nation's aids to navigation.

vault – A storage container for oil.

veteran – One who has been a member of the armed forces.

watch room – A space in or below the lantern of a lighthouse where the keeper could prepare the lamps during the night.

whale oil – A synonym for sperm oil. In the 1850s the price of whale oil quadrupled, prompting a search for an alternate fuel. Experiments proved that lard oil worked well when burned at high temperatures. The larger lamps were gradually switched from whale oil to lard oil.

whitewash – A mixture of lime and water used to whiten walls.

Further Reading ॐ

Carse, Robert, *Keepers of the Lights* (New York: Charles Scribner's Sons, 1969). One of the most readable of the many books about lighthouses.

Clifford, J. Candace and Mary Louise, *Nineteenth-Century Lights: Historic Images of American Lighthouses* (Alexandria, Virginia: Cypress Communications, 2000). A collection of 230 images illustrating the evolution of lighthouses during the 1800s.

DeWire, Elinor, *Guardians of the Lights* (Sarasota, Florida: Pineapple Press, 1998).

Holland, Ross, *American Lighthouses, An Illustrated History* (New York: Dover Publications, 1972). Probably the most comprehensive history of our nation's lighthouses.

The Lighthouse Encyclopedia (Norwalk, Conneticut: The Eaton Press, 2004).

National Maritime Initiative, *1994 Inventory of Historic Light Stations* (Washington, D.C.: National Park Service, 1994), available at <www.cr.nps.gov/maritime/ltsum.htm>.

Small, Constance Scovill, *Lighthouse Keeper's Wife* (Orono, Maine: University of Maine Press). Description of daily life in a lighthouse during the 20th century.

U.S. Coast Guard Historian's Office website provides a wealth of information on lighthouses including an extensive bibliography at <www.uscg.mil/hq/g-cp/history/h_LHbib.html>

U.S. Lighthouse Society, *The Keeper's Log* (San Francisco, California: quarterly publication).

Williams, Elizabeth Whitney, *A Child of the Sea* (St. James, Michigan: 1905 edition reprinted by Beaver Island Historical Society, 1983 and 2005).

Bluff Point Lighthouse on Lake Champlain, New York, was kept by Mary Herwerth from 1881 to 1901. Courtesy of National Archives, #26-LG-11-20.

Index ꗏ

Black Rock Light Station 6–10
Blackistone Island Light Station 78–83
Bluff Point Lighthouse 124
Bombay Hook Light Station 18–20
Bombay Hook Wildlife Refuge 20
bowsprit 40, 117
Brewerton, George 43
Bridgeport, Connecticut 6, 9
British Navy 2
Brown, Albert Gallatin 27
Brown, Captain Albert 89
Brumfield, Georgianna Crouch 109
buoy tenders 16, 25, 48, 99, 117. *See also* lighthouse tender
buoys 16, 82, 113, 117. *See also* bell buoy
Burges, Nathaniel 4
Burgess, Abbie. *See* Grant, Abbie Burgess

C

caisson 118
California 31–37, 59–62, 75–77, 84–92
California Gold Rush 59
Calumet Harbor Entrance Light Station 57–58
Cape Cod bungalow 31, 33
Cape Horn 75
Cape Mendocino 85
Carnegie Hero Fund 46
Carquinez Strait 85
Carquinez Strait Lighthouse 88
cast iron 27, 93, 94, 121
Central Hudson Steamboat Company 69
chandelier 12, 21, 118
channel lights 118
Chesapeake and Delaware Canal 113
Chesapeake Bay 108–114
cistern 21, 60, 75, 106, 118
Civil Service 70, 109, 118
Civil War 16, 20, 27, 39, 85, 105
Clifton, steamboat 40
Coffee, Kate. *See* McDougal, Kate
Colfax, Harriet 49–56, 109
Colfax, Schuyler 46, 49
collector of customs 28, 31, 63, 101, 118, 122

H

I

J

K

L

U.S. Navy 120
U.S. Revenue Cutter Service 121
U.S. Treasury Department 4, 11, 121

V

Van Riper, Clement 71
vault 8, 122
veteran 11, 31, 105, 122

W

Walker, Jacob 94, 98
Walker, John 94, 98
Walker, Kate 93–99
Walker, Mamie 98
War for Independence 2
War of 1812 11
Washington, George 4
Washington Territory 75, 76
watch room 27, 34, 70, 122
weather 109, 111. *See also* fog; storms
whale oil 2, 7, 15, 32, 122
Whitehead Light Station 21, 25
whitewash 19, 92, 110, 122
Whitney, Elizabeth. *See* Williams, Elizabeth
wick 55, 122
Williams, Bion 59
Williams, Daniel 74
Williams, Elizabeth 71–74
Williams, Frank 61
Williams, Johnson 59, 61
Williams, Julia 59–62
Wilson, Ellen 100–102
World War II 77, 111

Y

Younghans, Maria 27, 29–30
Younghans, Miranda 27, 29–30
Younghans, Perry 29